# *Your*
# *ETERNAL*
# *Reward*

*Triumph and Tears at the
Judgment Seat of Christ*

# Your
# ETERNAL
# Reward

# Erwin W. Lutzer

**MOODY PUBLISHERS**
CHICAGO

All Scripture quotations, unless indicated, are taken from the *New American Standard Bible,* © 1960, 1962, 1963, 1968, 1971, 1972, 1973, 1975, and 1977 by The Lockman Foundation, La Habra, Calif. Used by permission.

Scripture quotations marked (NKJV) are taken from the New King James Version. Copyright © 1979, 1980, 1982 by Thomas Nelson, Inc. Used by permission. All rights reserved.

Scripture quotations marked (NIV) are taken from the *Holy Bible: New International Version®.* NIV®. Copyright © 1973, 1978, 1984 by International Bible Society. Used by permission of Zondervan Publishing House. All rights reserved.

Scripture quotations marked (KJV) are taken from the King James Version.

ISBN-10: 0-8024-4192-0
ISBN-13: 978-0-8024-4192-8

We hope you enjoy this book from Moody Publishers. Our goal is to provide high-quality, thought-provoking books and products that connect truth to your real needs and challenges. For more information on other books and products written and produced from a biblical perspective, go to www.moodypublishers.com or write to:

Moody Publishers
820 N. LaSalle Boulevard
Chicago, IL 60610

*Printed in the United States of America*

*To my wife,*
*Rebecca Anne,*
*whose love for Christ*
*and thoughtful service to others*
*makes all who know her*
*convinced that "her reward shall be great"*

# CONTENTS

# $\mathscr{T}$EARS IN HEAVEN

T ears in heaven!

In the minds of many Christians, *tears* and *heaven* simply do not belong together. Like war and peace, light and darkness, health and sickness, these simply cannot coexist.

But I believe there are good reasons why there will be tears in heaven. When we reflect on how we lived for Christ, who purchased us at such high cost, well might we weep on the other side of the celestial gates. Our tears will be those of regret and shame, tears of remorse for lives lived for ourselves rather than for Him who "loves us, and released us from our sins by His blood" (Revelation 1:5). Perhaps we would never cease crying in heaven if God Himself did not come and wipe the tears from our eyes (Revelation 21:4).

The judgment seat of Christ is, to our shame, almost universally ignored among Christians. Most whom I have talked with think it will not be a very significant event. When I ask why, I usually get one of several reasons, often based on some misconceptions that have found their way into the minds of so many.

False assumptions die hard. I discovered that I could not teach the subject of the judgment seat of Christ until I had dislodged some impressions that had largely emptied this doctrine of its significance. Until we are willing to set aside these opinions, we will not be able to appreciate the rich teaching of the Bible on this topic. Nor will we be transformed by a doctrine that should impact our daily lives.

Here are some common assumptions which must be challenged if we are to recapture the biblical teaching on the judgment seat of Christ.

## MISCONCEPTIONS

Leading the list of mistaken ideas is the belief that there cannot be a serious review of our lives at the judgment seat of Christ because as believers our sins are forgiven and "cast . . . into the depths of the sea" (Micah 7:19). After all, the argument goes, as far as God is concerned, our past failures and sins do not exist. "Doesn't Calvary cover it all?" a friend of mine asked when I suggested that some people might experience deep regret along with lost privileges at the judgment seat of Christ. For him, the judgment seat of Christ is really no judgment at all. All believers will pass the judgment seat with flying colors.

Not so.

Let us hear the words of Paul. "For we must all appear before the judgment seat of Christ, that each one may be recompensed for his deeds [done] in the body, according to what he has done, whether good or bad" (2 Corinthians 5:10). That phrase, "whether good or bad," rids us of the cherished hope that our failures can never return to haunt us. It reminds us that our Father in heaven judges us even though we are secure in the knowledge that we are His children forever.

Recall the story of Ananias and Sapphira, who lied about the price of some property they had sold so that they might withhold a percentage of the proceeds while pretending to give all the money to the church (Acts 5:1–11). Though they were Christians, they were smitten by God and instantly died for their dishonesty. Perhaps when they arrived in heaven they might have said to themselves, "How could this have happened? Peter told us that Calvary covered it all!"

This experience of Ananias and Sapphira, along with others like it in the New Testament, is a powerful reminder that *God judges justified sinners.* And if He judges us on earth, sometimes even to the point of physical death, it is certainly not difficult to believe that He will judge us in heaven for the way we lived here. As Jim Elliff says, "Such warnings virtually bleed from the pores to Scripture." So it is.

King David, who committed the twin sins of adultery and murder, was judged for his sin even after he had confessed it and was assured of God's forgiveness. Nathan said: "The Lord also has taken away your sin; you shall not die. However, because by this deed you have given occasion to the enemies of the Lord to blaspheme, the child also that is born to you shall surely die" (2 Samuel 12:13–14). If Ananias and Sapphira remind us that God judges us for unconfessed sin, David reminds us that *God judges us for sins that have been confessed and forgiven.* Judicial forgiveness is one thing, but the discipline the Father inflicts on His wayward children is quite another.

Yes, those who trust Christ alone for their salvation are redeemed, eternally forgiven, and legally perfect before God. We are not under condemnation but have "passed out of death into life" (1 John 3:14). We enter heaven with the righteousness of Christ credited to our account; we are accepted on the basis of His worthy merit. To this all Christians must say "Amen."

But—and this is important—we should not conclude that every Christian will do well at the judgment seat of Christ. We can suffer serious loss; many of us might stand in shame before Christ as we see our lives pass before us. It is not true, as some teach, that ten minutes after our personal confrontation with Christ our meeting will have little significance because all of us will essentially receive the same reward. What happens at the judgment seat can have permanent consequences.

There are degrees of punishment in hell and degrees of reward in heaven. This does not mean that heaven will be divided into the haves and the have-nots. Eventually, everyone will be happy in heaven because God will comfort us by wiping the tears from our eyes. Everyone will be a servant and enjoy the fellowship afforded to all who enter the presence of God through Christ. But we shall not all have the same privileges, for the way we live will have a ripple effect that will go on for an eternity. Paul did not see a contradiction between teaching justification by faith and the related fact that we shall be judged for all our "deeds [done] in the body" since our conversion. The hows and whys will be explained in later chapters.

A second misconception is the belief that even after we have been converted our works have no merit before God. When the Reformers preached (and rightly so) that we are saved by grace alone and not by works, some theologians went on to say that our works after salvation are also nonmeritorious. They concluded that in heaven all Christians will either receive the same reward, or else any differences will be due to God's sovereign will. Many Bible students since that time have accepted the same basic premise.

Almost all Christians agree that some believers will receive the approval of Christ, whereas others will receive censure and disapproval; nevertheless, it is argued, any negative consequences will soon be forgotten. If some would have a different status in heaven, the argument goes, that would imply that works had some merit which God accepted, and this, it is said, would be contrary to the grace of God.

Let us test this premise.

Of course, I passionately agree that when we put our faith in Christ we are declared righteous by God because of Christ and not because of our works. Our deeds before our conversion are of no merit in the sight of God. "For by grace you have been saved through faith; and that not of yourselves, it is the gift of God; not as a result of works, that no one should boast" (Ephesians 2:8–9). If anyone reading this book thinks that he will be saved because of human effort, he will be tragically disappointed for all of eternity.

But works done *after* we have received the free gift of eternal life are special to God. Indeed, the same passage (quoted above) that affirms we are saved by faith alone because of grace continues: "For we are His workmanship, created in Christ Jesus for good works, which God prepared beforehand that we should walk in them" (v. 10). These works are sought by God and honor Him. We should strive to please Him, and for such works we shall be rewarded. Although we shy away from thinking that something we do has merit, Christ did not hesitate to promise that those who performed sacrificial acts would be "repaid" (Luke 14:14).

Melanchthon, Luther's confidant and a theologian in his own right, made an important distinction between works prior to salvation, which lack merit, and those after conversion, which he calls meritorious. He wrote:

> We teach that good works are meritorious—not for the forgiveness of sins, grace, nor justification (for we obtain these only by faith) but for other physical and spiritual rewards in this life and in that which is to come, as Paul says (1 Corinthians 3:8), "Each shall receive his wages according to his labor." Therefore there will be different rewards for different labours. . . . There will be distinctions in the glory of the saints.[1]

Of course, the works we do after our conversion do not have merit in and of themselves; they have merit only because we are joined to Christ. He takes our imperfect works and makes them acceptable to the Father. Also, we should not think that God must pay us like an employer who has a legal obligation to pay his employee. As we shall learn later, our good deeds are done only because God gives us the desire and ability to do them. They are a gift of His grace to us. Furthermore, no child is expected to work for his inheritance; indeed, it is not possible that he could "earn" all that the Father is pleased to give him.

But—and this must be stressed—the father *tests* his son to prove him worthy; the father uses that which is least to see if his child can be trusted with a greater share of the inheritance. *Dependability on earth translates into greater responsibility in heaven.* Just so, Christ will judge us on the basis of our worthiness, and thus our present faithfulness or lack thereof will have eternal, heavenly repercussions!

This does not mean that rewards are based on a day's pay for a day's work. God will reward us out of proportion to the work we have done. Though it appears that He would have no reason to reward us, He has placed Himself under a loving obligation to do so. If He didn't reward us, the author of Hebrews says, He would be "unjust." "For God is not unjust so as to forget your work and the love which you have shown toward His name, in having ministered and in still ministering to the saints" (Hebrews 6:10).

When we consider that the ultimate reward is to rule with Christ as a joint-heir, charged with the responsibility of authority over all God's possessions, it is clear that rewards are never earned in the usual sense of the word. God has obligated Himself to give us rewards, but this is strictly because of His grace. We can demand nothing; indeed, after we have done our best we are still unworthy servants, having "done only that which we ought to have done" (Luke 17:10). God has chosen to give us what we have no right to either demand or expect. *We are rewarded because of His generosity, not His obligation.*

A third and final misconception is that it is selfish to think of rewards as a proper motivation to serve Christ. After all, the argument goes, we should serve God out of love, and love alone. Shouldn't a basketball player give his best just for the sheer love of the game?

Furthermore, I have heard it said, "Will we not cast our crowns before Him anyway?" implying that we will give up our rewards and they will not mean anything beyond our initial meeting with Christ. This is based on the assumption (false, in my opinion) that the rewards are nothing more than the crowns themselves. Certainly rewards are sometimes spoken of symbolically as crowns, but the rewards themselves have to do with levels of responsibility that will be given to us. Regardless of what we do with our crowns, our rewards will reach into eternity.

Of course, it is quite right that we should serve God simply because He is God and worthy of our devotion. Yes, we should serve Him because we love Him rather than wanting a better position in the kingdom. Servants should simply serve, expecting nothing in return. But, as we shall see, there is more than one motivation for serving Christ. Love is one; fear, another.

Another motivation for serving is a strong desire that we would please Christ, who is eager to share His inheritance with us. It is not selfish to want Christ's approval. He wants us to win the right to rule with Him in the kingdom, and that should be our passionate yearning. A basketball player who loves the game will give his best, but he would be especially motivated if he knew the coach whom he loves had chosen to openly reward the faithful.

Let's not overlook the connection Paul makes between pleasing Christ and doing well at the judgment seat of Christ. "Therefore also we have as our ambition, whether at home or absent, to be pleasing to Him. *For* we must all appear before the judgment seat of Christ" (2 Corinthians 5:9–10, italics added). I would like to hear Christ say, "Well done, thou good and faithful servant" (Matthew 25:21, KJV), and I believe you would too. I would like to live in such a way that Christ would count me worthy to rule with Him. You feel the same way. Obviously no credit goes to us; in heaven, ruling with Christ will have no overtones of pride and self-seeking. But being found worthy to rule because we love Christ was Paul's desire and should be ours.

Christ often and unapologetically motivated the disciples with the prospect of rewards. He told them that they should put their treasures in heaven where their money would have more security and a better rate of return. "But lay up for yourselves treasures in heaven, where neither moth nor rust destroys, and where thieves do not break in or steal" (Matthew 6:20). In a future chapter we shall see that He often promised them that if they were sacrificially obedient their "reward will be great" (Luke 6:35; see also 6:23; Hebrews 10:35).

Think of the biblical saints who were driven to serve Christ because of the prospect of a reward. Abraham was willing to leave Ur and live in tents, "for he was looking for the city which has foundations, whose architect and builder is God" (Hebrews 11:10). He died without having received the promise, but it was this promise that motivated him to obey God. He was rewarded in the life to come.

Moses was willing to leave the treasures of Egypt, "choosing rather to endure ill-treatment with the people of God, than to enjoy the passing pleasures of sin; considering the reproach of Christ greater riches than the treasures of Egypt; for he was looking to the reward" (Hebrews 11:25–26). A careful calculation made him realize that it made sense to give up the visible earthly reward for the invisible future reward. Anyone who exchanges a lesser reward for a greater one is wise.

Paul feared that he might fail and thus be disqualified in the race of life (1 Corinthians 9:27). He urged believers in Philippi to prove themselves to be blameless in this perverse generation, "holding fast the word of life, so that in the day of Christ I may have cause to glory because I did not run in vain or toil in vain"

(Philippians 2:16). He was motivating them to do well "in the day of Christ." In fact, he wanted "cause to glory" in the life to come.

Christians who piously avoid any suggestion that the prospect of rewards should motivate us would be wise to admit their mistake and take up the challenge of Jonathan Edwards:

> Resolved: To endeavor to obtain for myself as much happiness in the other world as I possibly can, with all the power, might, vigor and vehemence, yea violence, I am capable of, or can bring myself to exert, in any way that can be thought of.[2]

I agree with Iosif Ton, who points out that rewards are not decorative medallions in which we can take pride. "The deepest reward is in the very fact that we will become what our Creator intends us to become. It is the reward of being made into the likeness of Christ. When we will be like Him, we will be qualified to share with Him in the inheritance, and to work with Him in important positions of high responsibility over the whole universe."[3] Our rewards are a continuation of our responsibilities begun on earth.

I am convinced that those who have been unfaithful will suffer serious loss. I agree with A. J. Gordon, who wrote, "I cannot think of a final divine reckoning which shall assign the same rank in glory, the same degree of joy to a lazy, indolent and unfruitful Christian as to an ardent, devoted, self-denying Christian."[4] If this life is a training ground for greater responsibilities, believers will be thoroughly judged; then once eternity begins they will differ in glory as lightbulbs differ in brightness.

Hell will not be the same for everyone, and heaven

will not be the same for everyone. The way we live here will have eternal, unchangeable, and profound consequences. The cup of cold water given in the name of Christ will not be forgotten; nor will the impure, self-indulgent Christian inherit the full blessings of the kingdom.

Earl Radmacher says that "the person I am becoming today, is preparing me for the person I shall be for all of eternity." Much will change about us in eternity, but much shall also remain the same. We will be the same people we were here on earth, though with a new nature and eventually a new body. And because our position in eternity will be momentous, the life I live today is momentous—*eternally* momentous! *Only in this life can we impact our eternity.*

We must pause long enough to let the reality of standing before Christ sink into our consciousness. Just Christ and you. Just Christ and me.

## TWO JUDGMENTS

To be clear, we must distinguish between two different judgments. Each involves a different group of people, each occurs at a different time, and those who are judged have a radically different destination.

The judgment seat of Christ, to which I have already referred, will take place when Christ returns to take all believers to be in heaven with Him. The purpose of this judgment will be to evaluate us so that we can be properly rewarded for the way we have faithfully (or unfaithfully) served here on earth. All who appear at this judgment will be in heaven, but the question that needs to be settled is the extent of our rule (if any) with Christ. This judgment is the subject of this book.

In contrast, the Great White Throne Judgment convenes many years later, just before the final phase of eternity begins. All who appear here will be thrown into the lake of fire, or what is called hell. The purpose of this judgment is to assess the degree of punishment that will be experienced for all of eternity. (I discuss this judgment briefly in chapter 10 of this book.)

There is a popular notion that we will appear before God to determine whether we will go to heaven or hell. But there is no such judgment mentioned in the Bible. Whether we go to heaven or hell is determined already in this life. At death, those who know Christ as Savior go directly to heaven where the judgment seat of Christ will take place; those who do not know Him go to a place called hades and will eventually be brought before God at the Great White Throne Judgment. Either way, everyone will encounter God.

That you will appear before God is more certain than the sunrise. And the judgment at which you will be summoned is determined in this life, based on your relationship with Christ. There is no opportunity to reroute your travel plans after you have died. One minute after you die your eternal destination is unalterably fixed.

Standing at the Great White Throne Judgment will be hordes from every country of the world, from every religion in the world, with the best intentions in the world. They will learn too late that God is serious about justice, and if Christ does not bear their punishment, they must bear their own. And since it is not possible for them to now accept Christ on the other side of death, they will be "thrown into the lake of fire" (Revelation 20:15).

If you are not sure at which judgment your name will be called, you still have the opportunity to settle the matter. You must admit your sinfulness and transfer all of your trust to Christ alone, for only He can fit you for heaven. "He who believes in the Son has eternal life; but he who does not obey the Son shall not see life, but the wrath of God abides on him" (John 3:36).

In fact, if you want more information on how to be sure of heaven, I suggest you skip to chapter 10. I've included the terrifying biblical description of the Great White Throne Judgment, along with an explanation of how you can avoid this frightful event. Take time to make your peace with God *now*.

## THE PURPOSE OF THIS BOOK

For several years I pondered the possibility of studying the judgment seat of Christ, or what is called the *doctrine of rewards*. It is with sobriety and not a little trepidation that I have finally had the courage to preach and write about this subject. The fact that you and I will be one-on-one with Christ, and He shall review our lives, is enough to give us pause.

The thesis of this book is that *the person you are today will determine the rewards you will receive tomorrow*. Those who are pleasing to Christ will be generously rewarded; those who are not pleasing to Him will receive negative consequences and a lesser reward. In other words, your life *here* will impact your life *there* forever.

If the knowledge that we will give an account to Christ "for [the] deeds [done] in the body, . . . whether good or bad" (2 Corinthians 5:10) does not motivate us to faithful living, it is quite possible that nothing else will. Here at last we must own up to the question of how much we really do love Christ. In that day there will be no place to hide.

Resist the temptation to think about how others might fare while standing in Christ's presence. Indeed, no doctrine should make us more hesitant to judge our brothers and sisters, for we shall stand before the same Christ as they. Let us not think we can do God's work of judgment for Him. There is a place for church discipline, but there is no place for a critical, unforgiving, judgmental spirit.

Also resist the temptation to hide behind a preconceived theological bias that would render the judgment seat of Christ of little consequence. Read with an open mind, willing to grapple with the full impact of what God has revealed. Along the way we will continue to expose those misinterpretations that have weakened the biblical teaching on the subject.

Join me on a journey that will challenge your thinking and, I pray, change your life. Let's prepare for that day when you and I will be alone with Christ; just reality and no pretense. Matthew Henry wrote, "It ought to be the business of every day to prepare for our last day."

Let's begin the journey.

## NOTES

1. Quoted in Iosif Ton, "Suffering, Martyrdom and Rewards in Heaven" (Th.D. diss., Evangelische Theologische Facultiet, Haverlee/Leuven, Belgie, 1996), 477.

2. Quoted in Jim Elliff, "The Starving of the Church," *Reformation and Revival: A Quarterly Journal for Church Leadership* 1, no. 3 (1992): 116.

3. Ton, 280.

4. See also A. J. Gordon, *Ecce Venit: Behold He Cometh* (New York: Revell, 1889), 271.

# CHAPTER TWO

# *Y*OU'LL BE THERE

**I**magine staring into the face of Christ! Just the two of you, one-on-one! Your entire life is present before you. In a flash you see what He sees.

- No hiding.
- No opportunity to put a better spin on what you did.
- No attorney to represent you.
- The look in His eyes says it all.

Like it our not, that is precisely where you and I shall someday be. *"For* we must all appear before the judgment seat of Christ, that each one may be recompensed for his deeds in the body, . . . *whether good or bad"* (2 Corinthians 5:10, italics added).

The judgment seat of Christ is often called the *Bema* (the Greek word for judgment seat used by Paul in 2 Corinthians 5:10, quoted above). Literally, the *Bema* refers to a raised platform that was used for the assembly where speeches were given and crowns were awarded to the winners. In ancient Rome the Caesars sat on a tribunal to award those who had made heroic contributions in winning the battle.[1] The *Bema* of Christ dwarfs all other tribunals, for here we shall be called into account before the all-knowing Judge.

Think this through: God gives us the faith by which we believe in Christ, and yet for this faith He gives us the gift of eternal life. God then works within us so that we might serve Him, and for our service He honors us with eternal rewards or *privileges*. Of course we don't deserve those rewards! But we are the sons and daughters of a loving Father who is more benevolent than we could possibly expect Him to be. He delights in giving to those who do not deserve His love.

"I'll be content to sit in the back row!" a friend of mine quipped when I brought up the subject of rewards in heaven. Looked at in one way, he echoed the sentiment of all of us. I interpreted his remark as a genuine expression of humility, the deep conviction that we deserve absolutely nothing. To have a seat in heaven, even if in the farthest corridor, is to enjoy an undeserved honor indeed. Anyone who feels differently has not yet seen his sinfulness before God!

But considered in a different light, his remark might betray a serious misunderstanding of the nature of rewards. What if those who "sit in the back row" are there because they have displeased Christ in their earthly sojourn? What if it was the Father's good pleasure to have us "sit in the front row," but we forfeited this privilege because of carnal living? Let us keep in mind that the idea of rewards is not ours; it is the Father's desire to bless us beyond all human reason. *We should be all that we can be on earth so that we can be all that we could be in heaven!*

I agree with Jim Elliff, who has observed that the people who piously care so little about eternal rewards are often killing themselves trying to accumulate a great "reward" now. They profess to be content with a "little shack in heaven," but want a much bigger one on earth! The Bible teaches that there is nothing wrong with ambition, just as long as we focus it on heaven rather than earth.[2]

We do not desire rewards for the reward itself, but because rewards are a reflection of Christ's approval of us. It is not wrong to want to be in the front row if such an honor is reserved for those who hear Christ say, "Well done, thou good and faithful servant" (Matthew 25:21, KJV).

## CHARACTERISTICS OF JUDGMENT

Paul begins in 2 Corinthians 5:10, "For we *must* all appear before the judgment seat of Christ" (italics added). There is this similarity between the *Bema* and the Great White Throne Judgment: attendance at one or the other is required. There can be no exception, no special deferment. When God calls our name we will be there. We cannot hide, for God will *find* us; we cannot scheme to make ourselves look good, for God shall *see* us. We cannot excuse ourselves, for God *knows* us.

### We Will Be Judged Fairly

Who will judge us? This is the "judgment seat of Christ." Christ, who knows us completely, loves us in spite of ourselves. We are judged by our Savior. He who died to save us, now stands to judge us. Because we are judged by One who loves us, we know that our judgment will be tempered with mercy. We'll be judged by One who wishes us well rather than by one who is anxious to condemn us. The Christ of the throne is the Christ of the Cross.

Our Savior is also our Brother. He has invited us to join His family; we share the same Father; thus, our names have been called for fellowship at the family table. To Mary Magdalene, a woman who had been possessed by evil spirits, Christ said, "I ascend to My Father and your Father, and My God and your God" (John 20:17). This judge will be merciful and fair because His Father is our Father. This is family business.

Even so, if we are unfaithful here on earth, the judgment could be severe. Immediately after Paul says that we shall be recompensed for the deeds done in the body, whether good or bad, he adds, "Therefore knowing the fear of the Lord, we persuade men" (2 Corinthians 5:11). Interestingly, he connects the fear (or terror) of the Lord with the judgment seat of Christ. Some scholars who think that our judgment will be a positive experience for everyone teach that Paul must now be giving a warning to unbelievers. But obviously such an interpretation makes an unnatural break in Paul's thought. He knew that the judgment seat of Christ for some believers would be fearful indeed.

Christ often gives severe warnings to His redeemed Church. To the congregation in Ephesus, whom He loved, He said, "Remember therefore from where you have fallen, and repent and do the deeds you did at first; or else I am coming to you, and will remove your lampstand out of its place—unless you repent" (Revelation 2:5). Our Savior and Brother will administer only that which is right and just. But he will not wink at our disobedience. He does not play favorites nor step aside when meticulous adjudication is called for.

We can be quite sure that we will be judged only for what we have done since our conversion to Christ. The apostle Paul expected to do well at the judgment seat of Christ even though he had persecuted the church, jailing Christians in his preconversion days. Yet this man who claimed he was the chief of sinners said just before he died:

> For I am already being poured out as a drink offering, and the time of my departure has come. I have fought the good fight, I have finished the course, I have kept the faith; in the future there is laid up for me the crown of righteousness, which the Lord, the righteous Judge, will award to me on that day; and not only to me, but also to all who have loved His appearing. (2 Timothy 4:6–8)

These are encouraging words for those who have a sinful or criminal record extending back to their pre-conversion days. The question to be answered at the judgment is how we have behaved as one of God's sons. We'll not be judged on what we did from the time of our *first* birth, but on what we did since our *second* birth.

Also, we will discover that every believer had the same potential to receive Christ's approval of "well done." Rewards are based on our faithfulness to opportunities presented to us since our conversion.

## We Will Be Judged Thoroughly

When Paul says we shall "appear" at the judgment seat of Christ, he uses the Greek word *phaneroō*, which means "to be made manifest." The imagery is that we shall be "turned inside out." One Bible scholar,

Philip Hughes, says the word *manifest* means "to be laid bare, stripped of every outward facade of respectability, and openly revealed in the full reality of one's character. All of our hypocrisies and concealments, all our secret, intimate sins of thought and deed, will be open to the scrutiny of Christ."[3]

We will be judged "for [the] deeds [done] in the body, . . . whether good or bad" (2 Corinthians 5:10). The good deeds will be lovingly remembered. That cup of cold water given in the name of the Lord will not be forgotten. Those whom we helped who cannot repay us—such deeds will attract the attention of the judge. (Later we will be discussing in more detail exactly what Christ will be looking for when He investigates our lives.)

That which is "bad," or worthless, will most assuredly be a negative counterbalance for that which is classified as "good." Because Christ is omniscient, every single detail can be brought into the final verdict, with every motive and action accounted for in context. Everything hidden today will be relevant in that day.

We've all known churches that have split over one or more issues, sometimes doctrinal, sometimes personal. Some people want the pastor to stay; others are convinced he should leave. Rumors circulate from one member to another; telephone lines buzz with charges and counterclaims. Usually people are hurt on both sides and hidden animosities simmer for years to come.

The Corinthian church had the tendency to fight and bicker among themselves, just as we often do. In 1 Corinthians Paul admonishes them, "Therefore do not go on passing judgment before the time, but wait until the Lord comes who will both bring to light the things hidden in the darkness and disclose the motives of men's hearts; and then each man's praise will come to him from God" (1 Corinthians 4:5).

Some disputes must wait until the judgment seat of Christ for resolution. Of course, we should do all we can to see that these matters are settled in this life. But we all know that our best efforts often fail. We can judge a person's behavior, but we cannot judge his motives. To know who is right and who is wrong we shall have to wait for God. I shall return to this theme in a later chapter.

I'm told that there is a central location in the World Wide Web that records all the "visits" of millions of subscribers. Somewhere, there is a person who could tally every Web site you and I have ever contacted. On the Internet there is much that is good and helpful as well as that which is destructive and evil. Whether good or bad, our actions are recorded.

Just so, God has His vast information network. Everything we have done or said is known to Him. He can, if necessary, "download" the information at a moment's notice. And whatever He chooses to reveal to us, whether it be little or much, we will not dispute the facts. We won't need to ask for dates, times, and places, for all such details are known to Him.

Later I shall discuss the question of whether we will actually see our sins. For now, let me simply say that we can be sure that our sins will provide input into the evaluation. "If we would judge ourselves, we should not be judged" (1 Corinthians 11:31, KJV). Unconfessed sin, sin that we have rationalized and idolized, will play a special part in the revelation and judgment.

If this seems fearful, remember that this judgment is also comforting. We've all had the experience of being criticized unfairly, even by our friends. When our motives are misinterpreted, when lies are spread by those who would delight in our downfall, such experiences are difficult indeed.

At the *Bema* the false accusations leveled against you will be brought to light. Cruelty, gossip, and misunderstandings will be cleared up. The judgment will be as detailed as it has to be to satisfy justice. All the "he said" and "she said" arguments will cease. Here the specifics are finally revealed; nothing but facts, nothing but the truth—the whole truth and nothing but the truth. If you need vindication, you will have it; if you need to be shown that you were in error, you will have that too.

Woodrow Kroll says, "Just as day brings light from the sun to reveal the hidden things of darkness, so that day will bring light from the Son to reveal the hidden things of darkness done in our bodies. However, many hidden things which are good will be revealed as well. . . . It will be both a day of vindication and a day of disappointment."[4] No time will be needed to gather evidence; no jurors will be selected to hear the arguments. Every detail has been known by Christ from the foundation of the world.

We will not dispute the outcome. We will not disagree with Christ, not because we are afraid to, but because we will have no reason to! If we have a question, it will be answered, but it is more likely that we will be speechless. We will see what He sees and know that His verdict is eminently just.

## We Will Be Judged Impartially

When Paul outlined the principles by which God will judge us, he assured his readers that "there is no partiality with God" (Romans 2:11). Indeed, the judgment of God is according to truth, that is, according to reality. No special advantages are given to the wealthy; those who counted on perks and power in this life find themselves stripped of every crutch, all forms of manipulation. Every trapping of man will fade into insignificance in the presence of the One who discerns the "thoughts and intents of the heart" (Hebrews 4:12, KJV).

Nor will pastors and missionaries be given preferential treatment. Those who have given their lives to serve Christ, often at great personal sacrifice, might receive a greater reward, but they are judged by the same standard of faithfulness. In fact, those who teach the Word of God will be judged by "a stricter judgment" (James 3:1) because they were given greater responsibility. Every detail will be evaluated within its larger context.

Most of us live in houses or apartments that are beautifully kept on the outside. But inside there is a mixture of cleanliness and dirt; perhaps a neat den but a closet filled with junk. During the tornado season the walls of houses are often blown off and everything within the closets and drawers lies visible to those who walk by. Just so, Christ will walk through our lives that now will be without walls. He will inspect the *rubies* as well as the *rubble.* He will show us whatever might be relevant to the judgment at hand.

In the presence of Christ, our outer image will give way to the reality of our inner character. The color of our skin, the size of our income, and our fame or lack of it will suddenly be irrelevant. This is one courtroom in which no one has an advantage. The Judge will determine what we did with what He gave us.

George Whitefield was a famous English preacher who had a profound ministry here in the United States during the first Great Awakening. His preaching on

the new birth, coupled with an emphasis on predesti-
nation, caused both conversions and controversy. He
said that the only epitaph he desired for his tomb-
stone was

> Here lies George Whitefield;
> What sort of man he was
> The great day will discover

Although I'm told that Whitefield did not get his
wish to have these words on his grave, they are true
just the same. Only the judgment seat of Christ will
reveal the sort of man he really was. The newspapers
that criticized him will be silent. His biographers,
whether friend or foe, will not be recruited for the
final assessment. In the presence of Christ the opinions of men will be woefully irrelevant, whether critic
or admirer. The divine verdict is the only one that
matters.

## We Will Be Judged Individually

If you are familiar with church life, you know that
we have a strong tendency to judge one another
regarding dos and don'ts. We like to judge others in
questionable matters according to our own standard.
In the first century, the Roman church was practically
split over the question of whether it was proper to eat
meat offered to idols, or whether it was right to eat
meat at all. Paul stressed that we should not judge
each other in these matters; petty arguments must be
put aside. Listen to his words:

> But you, why do you judge your brother? Or you
> again, why do you regard your brother with con-

tempt? For we shall all stand before the judgment seat
of God . . . *so then each one of us shall give* account *of*
himself *to* God." (Romans 14:10–12, italics added)

Here again, Paul uses the word *Bema,* a reference
to our one-on-one encounter with Christ. Underline
that word *himself:* "Each one of us shall give account
of *himself* to God." You will give an account of yourself; I shall give an account of myself. We will not
have to speak in behalf of someone else. So let us
stop carping about others; before our own Master we
will each stand or fall.

Whenever I have been asked to sing in a choir, I try
to sing softly, embarrassed that I might be off pitch. I
can get by without being noticed, especially if there is
a strong bass section. What I would never do is sing a
solo! But when we stand before Christ, we will, figu-
ratively speaking, have to sing our own song. There
will be no comparisons with others; no one to cover
for us, no opportunity to point out that we have more
to show than someone else.

Will the judgment be private or public? I think it
probably will occur in the presence of others, including angels before whom Christ promised to confess
that we are His (Luke 12:8). Recall that in the parable
of the talents, the slave who hid his talent (*mina*) was
reprimanded and the king gave some important
orders. "And he said to the bystanders, 'Take the mina
away from him, and give it to the one who has ten
minas'" (Luke 19:24). Those who were present saw
what happened and actually played a role in taking
the mina away from one slave and giving it to another. The judgment was public indeed.

If you find this terrifying, take comfort in the fact
that it will not matter whether our friends are present

or not. For one thing, we will all be together; no one will be in a position to gloat, nor will there be much opportunity to be surprised. There will be some good and bad in all of us.

More important, I'm convinced that when we look into the eyes of Christ, what others think will not matter. A student giving a recital on the piano cares only what his teacher thinks. To a football player, the censure or affirmation of the coach means much more than the boos or cheers of the fans.

In the presence of Christ, we will be oblivious to those who are around us. The expression on His face will tell it all. The judgment will be very "up close and personal," but also public.

Since there are millions of Christians, some people have questioned whether it is possible for Christ to judge us individually. The point is that there would not be enough time for millions of encounters, especially if it is done in the seven-year period beginning at the Rapture and ending with the glorious return of Christ. But let us not limit Christ's ability. We do not know how long each judgment will take; also, research will not be needed to get all the facts. Christ can cause our entire lives to be present to us in a moment of time. There will be no files to shuffle, no witnesses that must be called to confirm the data.

## We Will Be Judged Graciously

If it is a mistake to think that our failures can never return to haunt us, it is equally an error to think that the purpose of the *Bema* is that God might vent His pent-up anger at our carnality and selfishness. No, that anger has been absorbed for us by Christ, who died on the cross. He bore our eternal punishment and was the target of God's righteous indignation on our behalf. Nor is the purpose of the *Bema* that we might do better next time. There is no "next time," since we will now serve Christ perfectly. At issue is neither payment for our sins nor God's desire to "even the score."

The purpose of the judgment seat of Christ is to properly evaluate us, to grade us so that our position in the coming kingdom is made clear. This life is like a college-entrance exam that helps us know where we shall be slotted in the kingdom of the coming King To quote Hughes again, this judgment "is not a declaration of gloom, but an assessment of worth, with the assignment of rewards to those who because of their faithfulness deserve them and a *loss* or withholding of rewards in the case of those who do not deserve them."[5]

Imagine a father who promises his son a ride in his personal airplane if only the lad will mow the lawn six weeks in a row. Six weeks later the boy's record is one of failure: he mowed the lawn only three times, skipped two weeks, and the last time only partially completed the job. The test period is over, and the father tells the boy what he should already know: his dream of taking a flight above his town will not come to pass.

The father is not angry, but saddened by the boy's lack of faithfulness. He does not formally "punish" his son for his negligence. He does, however, reprimand the son, and the boy must live with consequences of his unfaithfulness. He must stand by while another boy in the neighborhood responds to the same challenge and is rewarded with a Saturday morning flight. What hurts most, however, is the look on his father's face. All that is punishment enough.

Christ will not be angry, but disappointed. We will be "recompensed for [the] deeds [done] in the body, . . . whether [they be] good or bad." After the judgment is over and eternity begins, we will be denied privileges; perhaps some of us will not get to reign with Christ because of unfaithfulness.

If you feel distraught because of your sins and failures, take heart. All of us have experienced the depths of our own evil hearts and actions. As we shall discover, those sins that we judge through personal repentance will not be brought to light, except insofar as they will result in a loss of rewards. But those sins that we tolerate, the matters that are unresolved between us and God and His people—these will be the specific subject of review and judgment.

In the midst of failure there will be grace. I'm convinced that Christ will find some things for which we will receive reward. Paul says, "Then each man's praise will come to him from God" (1 Corinthians 4:5b). Perhaps there will not be much for which we are praised, but Christ will search the Cosmic Internet and find something for which He can commend us.

Despite our propensity to sin, every one of us can live a life that will receive the Lord's approval rather than His rebuke. Indeed, our struggle against sin, if successful, is worthy of reward. Today, in dependence upon Christ, we can live in light of that Great Day.

## LIVING IN LIGHT OF THE JUDGMENT

We've already learned some lessons that should affect the way we live. First, keep in mind that *this life is training for the next*. We are to be learning the rules of the kingdom; we are apprentices for something better. God's purpose is to mature us in faithfulness and service so that we will be a credit to Him on earth and a companion for Christ in heaven.

Second, *every day we live is either a loss or a gain so far as our future judgment is concerned.* How we live today will help determine the words we hear from Christ tomorrow. Remember, the person we are today will determine the rewards we receive in the future.

When Billy Graham was asked by Diane Sawyer how he would like to be remembered, sadness came across his face. "I would like to hear the Lord say to me, 'Well done, Thou good and faithful servant,' but I don't think He will."

Two thoughts came immediately to mind. First, I surmised that Billy Graham was being more humble than he had to be! Here is a man who has preached the gospel to more millions than any other man in history. I think of his grueling schedule, the pressures and the heavy responsibilities he has borne. "Of course, he will do well at the *Bema*," I speculated.

My second thought: If Billy Graham does not think he will receive Christ's approval, what hope is there for the rest of us? Surely, if rewards are based on results, Billy Graham will be somewhere at the head of the line.

But in this respect Billy Graham was quite right. When he stands before Christ, his fame will not influence the outcome. Nor will the adulation of millions affect Christ's personal evaluation. Nor the fact that hundreds of thousands have come to Christ through his ministry. Like Whitefield, the manner of man Billy Graham was *"that day shall declare."*

This leads us to a third lesson. *Rewards are not based on results or size of ministry.* Some of us have had more widespread influence than others. Many who have served in mission fields can claim but few converts after lives of hardship and intense personal cost. Others are called to vocations in factories, farms, and within the home; some serve for many years, others for few. We will not be rewarded by a scale that asks for the number of souls saved, the number of sermons preached, or the number of books written. Comparisons with someone else will be off-limits.

Nor will we be rewarded for the length of time we serve. New converts can also receive Christ's approval. We will be judged on the *basis of our loyalty to Christ with the time, talents, and treasures that were at our disposal.* In other words, we are judged for the opportunities that were given to us, be they few or many, great or small. All believers have the potential to be generously rewarded.

To some who perhaps did not expect to be rewarded but were diligent about their calling, Peter wrote, "As long as you practice these things, you will never stumble; for in this way the entrance into the eternal kingdom of our Lord and Savior Jesus Christ will be abundantly supplied to you" (2 Peter 1:10b–11). Others who did not live diligently, those who cared little about whether they were pleasing the Lord or not, will experience "shame at His coming" (1 John 2:28).

What is God's purpose for us in eternity? What rewards can we win or lose? What will Christ be looking for?

Keep reading.

## NOTES

1. Joe E. Wall, *Going for the Gold* (Chicago: Moody, 1991), 32.
2. Jim Elliff, "The Starving of the Church," *Reformation and Revival: A Quarterly Journal for Church Leadership* 1, no. 3 (1992): 115.

3. Philip Edgcombe Hughes, *Paul's Second Epistle to the Corinthians,* New International Commentary on the New Testament (Grand Rapids: Eerdmans, 1962), 180.

4. Woodrow Kroll, *Tested by Fire* (Neptune, N.J.: Loizeaux, 1977), 51.

5. Hughes, 182.

CHAPTER THREE

# WHAT WE CAN GAIN

Glance over my shoulder and read this letter that arrived in my mailbox:

> I know someone who has appeared in several X-rated films. Since then she has become a Christian. But she worries that since these films are irretrievable and have been distributed all over the world, the harm they are doing will continue even after she dies.
>
> Will this interfere with her salvation? In other words, how will she be able to share in the joy of heaven, while as a direct result of what she did on earth, others continue to sin? She feels that she is leaving a legacy of evil. Can you offer any consolation?

Yes, thanks to the promises of Scripture, I believe I can offer some consolation. First, her past life will not interfere with her salvation. Christ died for sinners, even terrible sinners—yes, even pornographers and criminals. Our great-grandfather Adam left a worse "legacy of evil" than this woman, but God covered him with the skin of animals to cover his shame. These skins were symbolic of the coming of Christ, who would be killed so that we could be clothed in His righteousness. Many people have ongoing consequences of sins committed in their preconversion days. Yet, we can be secure in God's forgiveness even when the consequences of our sin continue. This forgiveness is a free gift given to those who acknowledge their sinfulness and trust Christ alone for their salvation.

Second, yes, this lady can look forward to joy in heaven, for at the judgment seat of Christ she will only be judged for what she did since she was saved, not what was done in her preconversion days. Having been forgiven much, she can indeed love much, and therefore be rewarded much. In fact, quite possibly, this woman will get to sit alongside of Christ and rule with Him forever.

The gift of salvation is not a reward for *works,* but a reward for *faith,* a faith which God has actually given to us! But when we are rewarded at the *Bema,* it will be based on our works; it will be according to our loyalty. I don't mean to say that we will receive what we deserve; as we will repeatedly emphasize, we will receive *far more* than we deserve, for God abounds in loving-kindness. We will not be paid in the sense that we will receive a day's pay for a day's work, but we will be paid in the sense that God will give us a hundred times more than we deserve. As Woodrow Kroll says, "Rewards are a gracious wage."

If your employer handed you a check late Friday afternoon and said, "This is a gift," you might not be amused. The implication would be that you don't deserve it; the check is simply an expression of compassion. But if you received a certificate for a two-week vacation in Hawaii because you were top salesman for the month, you would have "earned" the trip even though the reward would be far out of proportion to your effort. Christ, as we have already learned, did not hesitate to say that the faithful would be "repaid" by the Father.

The prospect of being found worthy to rule with Christ is the subject of this chapter. What Christ enjoys by divine right, He is willing to share with us by divine mercy! Today we are invited to catch a glimpse of the high honor to sit on Christ's throne and participate with Him in ruling the universe. "And there shall no longer be any night; and they shall not have need of the light of a lamp nor the light of the sun, because the Lord God shall illumine them; and they shall reign forever and ever" (Revelation 22:5). The journey from here to there is a love story that begins in the past and will end in this most glorious future.

Many Bible teachers simply take it for granted that everyone who enters heaven will get to rule with Christ. But many other passages suggest that this reward will be given to those who proved to be trustworthy on earth; if everyone in heaven does rule, some will be given greater positions of responsibility. I believe that there is much to gain at the judgment seat of Christ; thus there is also much we can lose.

## THE LOVE STORY

To explain the whys and hows, I must describe this drama in three scenes. The plot begins in the Garden of Eden and ends in heaven. Stay with me as I summarize God's purpose for the human race in general and His own people in particular. Step-by-step we shall better understand God's ultimate intentions for us all.

And now the story.

## The Past: Adam and Eve

The story begins in the Garden of Eden, where God chose to create mankind in His own image. "Let Us make man in Our image, according to Our likeness; and let them rule" (Genesis 1:26).

Neither angels nor animals were created in the image of God; this was the privilege only of mankind. This means that we share God's communicable attributes: personality, wisdom, love, truth, justice. Also, it means that we have an amazing capacity for God-likeness. We can be more like God than any other creature.

Let us ponder the details.

God fashioned man from the dust of the ground and "breathed into his nostrils the breath of life; and man became a living being" (Genesis 2:7). Soon after, Adam began to name the animals and take charge of the earth, just as God commanded. Yet in this idyllic paradise, something—or rather someone—was missing. God said, "It is not good for the man to be alone" (v. 18). No matter how beautiful the creation, no matter how close the fellowship between the man and God, Adam was incomplete. "There was not found a helper suitable for him" (v. 20). So God set out to find a companion for him; more accurately, He set out to create the companion Adam needed.

Now when God created Eve, He did not create her from the dust of the ground. Right from the beginning He wanted to show the organic unity of the human race, the solidarity that exists between the members of the human family. He especially wanted to demonstrate the oneness of a man and his wife. So God formed Eve from Adam's rib so that he could say, "This is now bone of my bones, and flesh of my flesh" (v. 23).

The helper—the bride—was "found." She would meet her husband's needs but also get to rule with him over the creation. Notice the plural pronouns. The Lord said, "Let *them* rule over the fish of the sea and over the birds of the sky and over the cattle and over all the earth, and over every creeping thing that creeps on the earth" (Genesis 1:26, italics added). The woman was to be a co-ruler with Adam, exercising with him the dominion over all creation. She was to enjoy full partnership in the divinely ordered plan. Whatever Adam and Eve did, they were to do together.

Only humans have the concept of family. Angels were created individually; they were never babies who eventually grew up and became adults. Angels don't have cousins, grandparents, aunts, and uncles; they have no brothers or sisters. They have only a functional unity; that is, they exist for the common purpose of serving God. But there is no *organic* unity between them.

In contrast, Adam and Eve would beget children in their likeness. Cain would marry one of his sisters and have brothers and cousins. This solidarity is exactly what God needed to fulfill His eternal purpose. Stay with me on this.

To recap: Adam was the first man, and from him a bride was created who would be able to exercise dominion with him. God was intent on finding a help-mate suitable for him.

Sin ruined all of this. Adam and Eve fell into the devil's trap, and their right to rule was forfeited. Satan picked up the scepter and asserted himself as ruler of the world. But Adam did not lose his place as the head of the human family. Although we, as his descendants, would, I'm sorry to say, be dysfunctional in varying degrees, Adam would still be the representative of the human race. The image of God would be *effaced* but not *erased*.

The love story between Adam, Eve, and God was in difficulty. Instead of ruling the world, we as humans would now be ruled by the world. Disease, destruction, and death would be the legacy bequeathed to this planet. We would sow, but not be sure that we would reap; we would establish friendships, but would be overcome by jealously, mistrust, and hatred.

Thankfully, this is only the first chapter in the story. God will intervene to dispel the darkness and keep the romance alive.

## The Present: Christ and the Church

The Almighty was not content with the fellowship of the Trinity in eternity past. The Father, Son, and Holy Spirit were in eternal harmony in purpose and action; their relationship was beautiful and perfect. Yet apparently there was something missing—the fellowship of creatures would better display God's attributes. Mankind's plunge into sin would give God a gracious opportunity to showcase His love and intentions.

So the Almighty chose to clean up the mess Adam and Eve had created. Specifically, He had a Son named Christ, who would stand at the head of a whole new race of humanity. This Son is known as the "second Adam," for He will succeed where the first Adam failed. Adam was only a replica of God, but Christ is the perfect "image of the invisible God" (Colossians 1:15). Such a perfect image that He is, in fact, God.

Long before the Fall, God the Father promised a gift of redeemed humanity to His Son. The Son would purchase these people and they would be united as one body to share in His love and honor. And because this bride would be purchased at high cost by the Bridegroom, the intensity of the love would be evident for all to see.

Think this through. *Just as God sought a bride for Adam, so God sought a bride for His Son, Jesus Christ.* He chose to prepare a companion who would be able to share His Son's rule over the universe, someone who would enjoy His dominion. This bride would be loved, honored, and invited to join Christ on the throne of the universe.

Thanks to God, millions of people will belong to the number of the redeemed, united in one consciousness, one purpose, and one love. Just as the body is one and has many members, so also is the body of Christ: Many members all unified in one body; one bride for God's most beloved Son.

So Christ stands at the head of new humanity, a new family. When we are born into this world, we are born of the seed of Adam, which is called "corruptible seed" (1 Peter 1:23, KJV; "perishable," NASB). We share the nature of our fallen parents and grandparents. When we are "born again" (John 3:3, 7), we receive God's seed that we might be replicas of His Son. We are begotten of "incorruptible" seed, God's seed (1 Peter 1:23, KJV; "imperishable," NASB), so that we can be "partakers of the divine nature," members of God's own family (2 Peter 1:4). *We are to be like Christ to the extent that the finite can be like the infinite; we are as much like Him as the creature can be like the Creator.*[1]

What is God's purpose for us here and now? We, as God's chosen bride, are being prepared for future responsibilities. In the words of one writer, God's intention "is the production and preparation of an Eternal Companion for the Son, called the Bride, the Lamb's Wife."[2] We are being tested to see whether we are worthy of such responsibilities.

Intimacy between a husband and wife should mirror this divine agenda. As husbands, we are to showcase the beauty of our wives, just as God is going to put the church on display in "all her glory" (Ephesians 5:27). We are to recognize our wives as co-heirs, fulfilling the role Eve was to have over the earth. Read these familiar words with new appreciation:

> Husbands, love your wives, just as Christ also loved the church and gave Himself up for her; that He might sanctify her, having cleansed her by the washing of water with the word, that He might present to Himself the church in all her glory, having no spot or wrinkle or any such thing; but that she should be holy and blameless. (Ephesians 5:25–27)

We are not yet married to Christ, but we are engaged. During these days God is preparing us for the wedding. This is a time of purification, a time of testing and training. We are being primed for the coming marriage along with the rights and privileges that accompany it. Just as the bride is to enjoy the same honors as her husband, even so, the church inherits the honors of God's eternal Son.

And a greater chapter has yet to be written.

## The Future: The Bride Is Enthroned

We cannot have the honor of being a joint-heir with Christ unless we are His relatives. To participate in His title deed to the universe we must be members of His family.

We qualify because Christ is our brother. He came to Bethlehem not as an angel, but in the form of mankind. "For assuredly He does not give help to angels, but He gives help to the descendant of Abraham" (Hebrews 2:16). Christ had to become one of our relatives in order for God to shower us with the honors reserved for members of His family. Unless we were God's sons and daughters we could not legally receive the family inheritance.

God had one "only begotten Son" (John 3:16), but He longed for more sons, specifically sons who would be, at least in some respects, like His own.

> For it was fitting for Him, for whom are all things, and through whom are all things, in bringing many sons to glory, to perfect the author of their salvation through sufferings. For both He who sanctifies [Christ] and those who are sanctified [those whom Christ redeemed] are all from one Father; for which reason He is not ashamed to call them brethren. (Hebrews 2:10–11)

Let me stress one more time that we are brothers with Christ because we share the same Father. We all know how embarrassing a wayward brother can be to the rest of the family. One woman I know disowned her brother because he was such a reprobate! We might think that Christ would be chagrined to be called our brother, but He is not. No matter how badly we reflect on the family, He does not disown us. We share family privileges, and He loans us the family name. He loves His brothers and sisters. He delighted in bringing "many sons into glory."

In our earthly existence when a father dies, the

brothers and sisters share the family fortune. Of course, our Father in heaven does not die, but we do. And when we get to heaven, we are "heirs." When the title deed is read, we are partners; we share the Son's estate. "The Spirit Himself bears witness with our spirit that we are children of God, and if children, heirs also, heirs of God and fellow heirs with Christ, if indeed we suffer with Him in order that we may also be glorified with Him" (Romans 8:16–17).

If you are a believer, expect to hear your name when God's last will and testament is opened. Since we are joint-heirs, the will cannot be dispensed unless we receive our inheritance. As it turns out, Christ is "heir of all things" (Hebrews 1:2), and as His brothers and sisters we are fellow heirs in an eternal, heavenly existence. We do not know all that this inheritance includes.

Certainly every believer will have an eternal, indestructible body, just as Christ has; we will not be limited by distance or endurance. Also, every believer will have proximity to the Father, the ability to behold Him in all of His beauty, to spend an eternity studying the wonders of His attributes and purposes.

If we want to know more about our future existence, we must only look at Christ after the Resurrection. He had a beautiful and powerful body that masked radiant glory. All of His brothers and sisters will be like Him.

> See how great a love the Father has bestowed upon us, that we should be called children of God. . . . Beloved, now we are children of God, and it has not appeared as yet what we shall be. We know that, when He appears, we shall be like Him, because we shall see Him just as He is. (1 John 3:1–2)

We should not be surprised that John motivates us to pure lives in light of such a prospect. He continues, "And everyone who has this hope fixed on Him purifies himself, just as He is pure" (v. 3). Far from giving us license to sin, the grace of Christ should drive us to holiness. We should want to be like our Savior and brother.

Our famous brother does not keep us at a distance. He invites us to share His throne in the coming kingdom and beyond. We will be His bona fide partner, His judicial equal. We who are a gift from the Father to the Son, we who are the bride and eternal companion for the Son might well be startled by this promise, "To him that overcometh will I grant to sit with me in my throne, even as I also overcame, and am set down with my Father in his throne" (Revelation 3:21, KJV).

Let's take this slowly. As a reward for the Son's faithfulness, He was invited to sit on the throne of the Father. If we are overcomers, we are invited to sit with Christ on the Father's throne He rightfully inherited. So if the Son sits on the Father's throne and we sit on the Son's throne, are we not sitting on the throne of God?

At this point we have reached the limits of our comprehension; we cannot grasp what the text means. We understand the words, but the implications elude us. We can only listen with John, who heard these words from the throne: "He who overcomes shall inherit these things, and I will be his God and he will be My son" (Revelation 21:7). Surely we are in awe of the generosity of God.

Of course, we should never think that we shall either become God or take His place. There is no room in the Bible for the "potential divinity of man." No, God has picked us up from the pit of sin and lifted us to dizzy heights. We shall forever be the creature and He the Creator. This is not proof of man's greatness and potential, but rather an example of God's love and undeserved grace! *It has nothing to do with what we have been able to make of ourselves, but everything to do with what God has chosen to make of us!*

Angels, bless them, are not qualified to reign with Christ. For one thing they are not brothers to Christ, and therefore do not share in the family inheritance. For another, they were not chosen to be Christ's eternal companion. They do the will of God with joy and holy obedience, but they are not participants in God's plan for the Son to purchase a bride for Himself.

Let me say again: We shall be as much like Christ as it is possible for the creature to be like the Creator; as much as the finite to be like the infinite. We shall be co-rulers with Christ, sitting on His throne, bought by Him, loved by Him, and honored by Him. (What this might mean is discussed in more detail in chapter 9.)

## A Promise to the Faithful

Does the Bible teach that all believers will get to reign with Christ? Does it matter whether we train for heavenly rule? Will everyone inherit the kingdom equally? Will all the saints share an equal honor at the marriage supper of the Lamb?

God has always reserved special rewards for those who are most faithful. When Israel left Egypt, the nation had been redeemed by God. At least a remnant of those who died in the desert, as far as we know, will be in heaven. They were redeemed by the blood of the Lamb; they experienced redemption from Egypt. And yet they died without entering into the fullness of God's promise; they missed Canaan. The land was a promise of additional blessing for those who were faithful. Of the older generation, only Joshua and Caleb qualified.

Even Moses was excluded from the land of Canaan because of his disobedience. He will be in heaven, but he forfeited his earthly inheritance. In the Old Testament it was possible to be regenerate, belong to God, and still miss out on the extra blessing of inheritance. Salvation was a gift through faith, but the added blessing was dependent on obedience.

Today, we are not concerned about entering into the land of Canaan, but the same principle applies. Just as some did not enter into the land and yet made it to heaven, even so some will be in heaven but without experiencing the fullness of reward. Rewards are always dependent on faithfulness.

Paul made it clear that slaves were to serve their masters as they would serve Christ. If they were devoted, the Lord would give them *the reward of the inheritance.* Some would accept his challenge; possibly others did not.

> Whatever you do, do your work heartily, as for the Lord rather than for men; knowing that from the Lord you will receive the reward of the inheritance. It is the Lord Christ whom you serve. For he who does wrong will receive the consequences of the wrong which he has done, and that without partiality. (Colossians 3:23–25)

Slaves could accept unjust wages with the assurance that Christ would personally reward them for their faithfulness. Of course, if they could better their position, that would be acceptable, but they lived in a culture where there was no opportunity to redress the wrongs. But if slaves served their masters as if they were Christ, Christ would reward them. Their reward was dependent on their works.

All believers have God as their inheritance, but there is another inheritance, an additional one given to those who are faithful. All believers will get to be heirs, but they will not inherit the same things.

Christ made the same point to His disciples.

> Truly I say to you, that you who have followed Me, in the regeneration when the Son of Man will sit on His glorious throne, you also shall sit upon twelve thrones, judging the twelve tribes of Israel. And everyone who has left houses or brothers or sisters or father or mother or children or farms for My name's sake, shall receive many times as much, and shall inherit eternal life. (Matthew 19:28–29)

Imagine the payback! To leave father and mother for the sake of Christ is to receive "many times as much" and "inherit eternal life." Obviously eternal life is a gift given to those who believe on Christ, but the expression "inherit eternal life" apparently refers to an additional acquisition, something more than simply arriving in heaven. It refers to a richer experience of being appointed by Christ to be in charge of the affairs of the cosmos as a ruler or judge. Salvation is guaranteed to those who accept Christ by faith; rewards are not. Entering heaven is one thing; having a possession there is quite another. One is the result of faith; the other, the reward for faith plus obedience.

The Bible is a realistic book. It does not assume that all believers will be faithful. Indeed, there are many examples of unfaithfulness of believers. History itself proves that many true Christians have buckled under persecution and have even denied Christ to save their lives or the lives of their families. In fact, many deny

Christ just to save their jobs or their reputations. Others are seduced by the temptations of this world.

The Bible nowhere expressly says that some believers will not reign with Christ. However, the promises of reigning with Him are almost always explicitly tied to obedience, faithfulness, or being an overcomer. As Paul wrote in 2 Timothy 2:12, "If we endure, we shall also reign with Him; if we deny Him, He also will deny us." In the Revelation it says, "He who overcomes, and he who keeps My deeds until the end, to him I will give authority over the nations" (2:26).

Either some Christians will not get to rule with Christ or they will rule over a lesser territory. If we remember the parable of the talents, we will keep in mind that one unfaithful servant had his talent taken from him and given to another. While others reigned over cities, he did not. All that he could hope for was to be admitted into the kingdom; he could not inherit its most prized positions.

## WEDDING PREPARATIONS

Earlier I mentioned that we are engaged to Christ, but someday we will be married to Him. We have in the Bible a rather detailed description of the "marriage supper of the Lamb" (Revelation 19:9), for which we must be properly dressed. At every wedding in which I have participated, the attenders are always interested in what the bride is wearing. The style of the dress and the choice of flowers and veil are all the focus of attention. We read:

> "Let us rejoice and be glad and give glory to Him, for the marriage of the Lamb has come and His bride has made herself ready." And it was given to her to clothe

herself in fine linen, bright and clean; for the fine linen
is the righteous acts of the saints. (Revelation 19:7–8)

*The righteous acts of the saints!* What are these righteous acts? Certainly not the acts that declared us justified before God; we cannot stress too often that we
did not work for the garments of righteousness that
Christ gives us. These are different garments.

In order to attend the marriage supper of the Lamb,
we need two different suits of clothes. The first is the
righteousness of Christ, the gift which admits us into
heaven. This is a free set of clothes, the garments by
which we are ushered into heaven's courts. "He made
Him who knew no sin to be sin on our behalf, that we
might become the righteousness of God in Him"
(2 Corinthians 5:21).

But the second suit of clothes is a wedding garment
for the marriage supper. This suit is not the righteousness of Christ, but rather the deeds we have done for
Christ on earth. Christ has made us ready for heaven;
we must make ourselves ready for the wedding feast.
We must distinguish between what only God can do
and that which we can have a part in doing.

What are we doing today? We are sewing the garments that we shall wear at the marriage supper of the
Lamb. We are making sure that we will not be so
scantily clad that we shall be ashamed. John warns,
"And now, little children, abide in Him, so that when
He appears, we may have confidence and not shrink
away from Him in shame at His coming" (1 John 2:28).

If you ask how these garments became so "white
and clean," I reply that many of our imperfect works
are made perfect in the sight of God through Christ.
God takes what we do, and if it is done for Him, these
deeds are made white and clean. Just recently, a

woman died who was faithful to Christ throughout her long life. Many years ago I stopped by her house to run an errand, and as she came to the door, her face was flush with tears. She apologized for crying, explaining, "You caught me in the middle of my prayer time for my family." I think she was sewing a garment for the wedding; my suspicion is that she will be well clothed at the marriage supper.

The purpose of our trials and temptations is to train us for ruling with Christ. We are learning the laws of the kingdom, responding in faithful obedience. We are given the opportunity of becoming overcomers so that we might inherit the promises. "For momentary, light affliction is producing for us an eternal weight of glory far beyond all comparison" (2 Corinthians 4:17). Place all of your trials on one end of a scale and the eternal weight of glory on the other, and it will go "plunk"! It is the weight of a feather versus a cubic foot of gold!

A family I know lost both of their children to prolonged and severe battles with cancer. And now, as I write, the father himself is down to 125 pounds, expected to die at any time of the same disease. What is God's purpose in all of this? It is to increase the eternal joy of the saints. Not the present joy, to be sure, for the moment seems to be utterly devastating, but *we can only become overcomers when there is something that must be overcome!*

We want life to be smooth, secure, uninterrupted. God has a different agenda. He is purifying us, testing us, training us so that we might be presented to Him as a pure church, ready to take our place sitting next to Christ on His throne. The English preacher Spurgeon wrote: "O Blessed axe of sorrow that cuts a pathway to my God by chopping down the tall trees of human comfort."

Our desire to pass our test and receive Christ's approval is not prideful; rather, it motivates us to worship a God who would be so generous with His undeserving children. We can only wonder at Christ's gracious words: "Fear not, little flock; for it is your Father's good pleasure to give you the kingdom" (Luke 12:32, KJV). Let me repeat that the idea that we should reign with God's Son is not ours, but His. God's desire is to display His wonder and grace throughout all of eternity, "in order that in the ages to come He might show the surpassing riches of His grace in kindness toward us in Christ Jesus" (Ephesians 2:7).

In the next chapter we shall discuss in more detail what it means to "suffer loss." We will attempt to answer the question of what it might be like to enter into heaven minus the rewards reserved for the faithful.

We shall learn that if we are unwilling to suffer loss for Christ in this life, we shall surely suffer loss in the life to come. Let us examine our hearts lest we be among those who do not hear Christ's "Well done."

## NOTES

1. Paul Billheimer, *Destined for the Throne* (Fort Washington, Pa.: Christian Literature Crusade, 1975), 37. The author develops the concept that the ultimate goal of our trials on earth is that we be trained to eventually reign with Christ. Some of the ideas of this chapter were generated by the reading of this challenging book.
2. Ibid., 15.

## CHAPTER FOUR

# *W*HAT WE CAN LOSE

There is a story about a man who was trudging through a blistering desert. He was faint with thirst, and to his delight he came across a well with a pump. Next to the pump sat a small jug of water with a sign, "Please use this water to prime the pump. The well is deep so you will have enough water for yourself and your containers. Please fill the jug for the next traveler."

Should the man play it safe and drink the jug of water, assured that his parched lips would at least get some relief? Or should he take the risk of pouring the water down the pump in hopes of getting all he would need?

Do we believe God's promises that He will repay us if we take the risk of serving Him with a whole heart? Or do we live as if this is the only life that matters? Christ warns, "He who has found his life shall lose it, and he who has lost his life for My sake shall find it"

(Matthew 10:39). If I give up the control of my life to God, I shall find it; if I maintain control, I shall lose it.

If we think of heaven as a theme park, we must emphasize that the entrance ticket is free. Christ must be received by faith; we are saved "not of works, lest any man should boast" (Ephesians 2:9, KJV). But if we want to go on some of the rides, if we want to be rewarded and not be embarrassed at the sadness we cause Christ, we must be faithful on earth. The entrance is free, but some additional benefits are based on merit.

## THE JUDGMENT OF FIRE

Perhaps the most vivid picture of the judgment seat of Christ is Paul's metaphor given to the church at Corinth. He pictures a building with a strong foundation, capable of holding the weight of the walls and roof, but these materials must be tested. What kinds of substances were used in the building? Can this structure withstand the test of time? Only when the building is set aflame is the answer made clear. And yes, some builders will suffer loss.

Unfortunately, this passage has often been interpreted as a reference to carnal Christians who supposedly believed on Christ but lived lives of open fleshly rebellion. And yet, when they die, we are told, they will be in heaven, "saved as by fire." But Paul did not write this to give carnal Christians at least a bit of comfort. His point, I believe, lies in another direction.

He begins by saying that he cannot speak to the believers at Corinth as to spiritual men, but as to "men of flesh, as to babes in Christ" (1 Corinthians 3:1). But keep in mind that these believers were learning how to exercise their gifts, they were supporting the church and interested in spiritual growth. They were not modern carnal Christians who made a commitment to Christ in their youth, then wasted their lives in wanton sin. Their carnality revealed itself in the immaturity of putting their favorite man on a pedestal; some followed one leader, others another (vv. 3–4).

To address these petty jealousies, Paul uses two metaphors. The first is *agricultural:* "I planted, Apollos watered, but God was causing the growth" (v. 6). The praise is given to God's part in the work, namely, the miracle of life, the marvel of growth. Rewards are never far from Paul's mind, so he adds, "Now he who plants and he who waters are one; but each will receive his own reward according to his own labor" (v. 8).

Then, second, he presents an *architectural* metaphor. "According to the grace of God which was given to me, as a wise master builder, I laid a foundation, and another is building upon it, But let each man be careful how he builds upon it" (v. 10). He is speaking about the leaders who build churches; he is giving both warning and encouragement to those who have responsibility within the congregation.

Now we come to the crucial verses:

> Now if any man builds upon the foundation with gold, silver, precious stones, wood, hay, straw, each man's work will become evident; for the day will show it, because it is to be revealed with fire; and the fire itself will test the quality of each man's work. If any man's work which he has built upon it remains, he shall receive a reward. If any man's work is burned up, he shall suffer loss; but he himself shall be saved, yet so as through fire. (1 Corinthians 3:12–15)

Paul's point is that some leaders are trying to build the church with poor materials; they gather a congregation quickly, but there is nothing transforming about their ministry. They might work hard, but because their energy is misdirected, they will have nothing that lasts in glory.

Others are trying to build with precious stones; they have a ministry based on the Word of God, prayer, and the Spirit. They value character, which D. L. Moody defined as "what a man is in the dark." They know that they will be judged, not just for what they *did* but for who they *are*. As veteran missionary to India Amy Carmichael used to say, "The work will never go deeper than we have gone ourselves." These shall receive a reward.

The person who is "saved so as by fire" is indeed a Christian, but his leadership has been flawed. He has relied too heavily upon himself, his techniques, and his training. He did not approach the work with a spirit of dependence and faith; he did not do the work with Spirit-directed faithfulness. He will be "saved so as by fire."

Though Paul's point is intended for the leaders of the church, it can be applied to all of us. We are all building our lives, day by day; each of us will be tested, and each life will reveal a mixture of precious stones and stubble.

Imagine for a moment that all of our deeds were turned into either precious metals or trash, and then torched. The kind of life we lived would become evident by the size of the fire. The question would be: What was left when the flames died out? The more carnality and selfishness, the more "wood, hay, straw" and the less "gold, silver, precious stones." This metaphor helps all of us come to terms with the thoroughness of God's judgment.

## The Final Judgment of Sin

Will we actually see our sins at the judgment seat? Perhaps Hoekema is right when he suggests that the sins and shortcomings of believers will be "revealed as forgiven sins, whose guilt has been totally covered by the blood of Christ."[1] If so, we could see our sins, which would be represented to us as forgiven by God's grace.

What we do know is that Paul taught clearly that we will receive the consequences of our wrongs at the judgment. He reminded slaves to serve their masters as they would Christ, "knowing that from the Lord you will receive the reward of the inheritance" (Colossians 3:24). Then he adds, "For he who does wrong will receive the consequences of the wrong which he has done, and that without partiality" (v. 25). Even if our sins are represented as forgiven, we cannot escape the conclusion that our lifestyle is under judicial review, with appropriate rewards and penalties. We will suffer for our "wrongdoing." And even what is hidden will be brought to light.

The respected theologian John Murray, when speaking of the judgment seat of Christ, says that God will leave nothing at loose ends; in fact, since believers will be fully sanctified, they will desire such a judgment: "Besides, it is against the gravity of their sins that their salvation in Christ will be magnified, and not only the grace but the righteousness of God will be extolled in the consummation of their redemption."[2]

We should not think that the loss of rewards means that Christ takes from us something we once had. As Woodrow Kroll says, "We are not stripped of rewards as an erring soldier is stripped of his stripes."[3] We receive no heavenly rewards on earth, so there is nothing that can be taken away from us; only when we stand before our Master are rewards given out. But the absence of rewards is serious indeed.

If we do have rewards coming to us, no one can take them from us. Christ warned the church at Philadelphia, "I am coming quickly; hold fast what you have, in order that no one take your crown" (Revelation 3:11); He did not mean that someone can steal our reward. Indeed, Christ said that those who have treasures in heaven will *not* have them stolen. Christ warns, however, that we *can* forfeit our reward by default and by failing to use the opportunities God gives us. Someone else can take our crown only if we let him get in the way of our relationship with God.

Three descriptive phrases help us visualize just how thorough this judgment will be. Paul wrote that our works will "become evident," for the day will "show it" because it is to be "revealed with fire" (1 Corinthians 3:13). The imagery is that of a person who has his pockets turned inside out to reveal every particle of lint. We will watch as Christ does the revealing, the analyzing, the judging.

## The Kinds of Materials

Two kinds of materials are contrasted. We can find a pile of wood, hay, and stubble almost anywhere, especially in rural areas. Precious gems are quite another matter. Hold them in your hand, and they are of more value than mounds of wood and straw. So it is not how *much* we do for Christ, but rather *what* we do and *how* we do it. Of course, this does not mean that we should do as little as possible for Christ, insisting that we have made up for our slothfulness through "quality." Paul's point is simply that much of what we do, if done in the wrong way and for the wrong reasons, is worthless.

Why do our works have to be subjected to the flames? The natural eye cannot easily tell the difference between these building matcrials. Not even Paul was confident that he could always separate junk from gems. From our perspective, a believer might have nothing but an impressive pile of combustible material; but when torched, nuggets of gold might be found embedded in the straw. Conversely, what we thought was a gold brick of some notable saint might just be the end of a wooden beam. Only the fire can separate the real from the fake.

- Our thoughts and intentions will be judged. "For the word of God is living and active . . . and able to judge the thoughts and intentions of the heart. And there is no creature hidden from His sight, but all things are open and laid bare to the eyes of Him with whom we have to do" (Hebrews 4:12–13). We who are adept at hiding our true selves from others and even fooling ourselves, will suddenly have no place to hide. The piercing, probing, omniscient eyes of Christ will see through us.
- Our words will be judged. "And I say to you, that every careless word that men shall speak, they shall render account for it in the day of judgment" (Matthew 12:36). And that which is spoken in a bedroom will be shouted from the housetop, for "there is nothing covered up that will not be revealed, and hidden that will not be known" (Luke 12:2). Obviously, not everything said in our bedrooms will be shouted from the housetops. Christ is speaking of those sins we have covered

and refused to bring to Him in confession and repentance.

• Our motives will be judged. "But to me it is a very small thing that I should be examined by you, or by any human court; in fact, I do not even examine myself. I am conscious of nothing against myself, yet I am not by this acquitted; but the one who examines me is the Lord. Therefore do not go on passing judgment before the time, but wait until the Lord comes who will both bring to light the things hidden in the darkness and disclose the motives of men's hearts; and then each man's praise will come to him from God" (1 Corinthians 4:3–5).

If we should not pass judgment before the time, it can only be because the unresolved disputes among believers will be adjudicated at the *Bema*. There the injustices among God's children will be brought to light, truth will triumph, and the righteous will be vindicated. Consider:

• An American missionary organization raised money for property, including buildings, in a country of Europe. When the chairman of the European board resigned, a local board member was able to usurp authority, rewrite the constitution of the organization, and declare himself owner. This Christian leader, in effect, stole the property from the Christian organization, expelled its leadership, and put the church and newly built apartments in his name.

• A Christian couple had a bitter divorce. There were so many lies, deceptions, and deep hurts that counselors couldn't establish agreement on so much as a single point. The husband eventually abandoned his wife and children and yet used their names as dependents on his income tax forms.

It might be tempting to think that these Christians will walk through heaven's gates hand in hand, with old animosities forgotten. Yes, of course, at that time all believers will have new natures and will not be subject to grudges and bitterness. But this does not mean that what happened on earth will be hidden. Paul taught that the believers in Corinth should not think they have to settle every issue, but wait for Christ to do it. What is the purpose of exposing the secrets of the hearts if it is not to bring final reconciliation to unresolved disputes? (See 1 Corinthians 4:3–5, quoted above.)

If you have had your reputation ruined by a vindictive believer, take comfort in the fact that the truth shall some day be revealed. Is not the *Bema* the place where injustices on earth shall finally be addressed? Is not this why Paul said we should not take revenge but leave the matter with God? "Never take your own revenge, beloved, but leave room for the wrath of God, for it is written, 'Vengeance is Mine, I will repay,' says the Lord" (Romans 12:19).

Christ will untangle the disputes that baffled us on earth. He will bring to light "the things hidden in the darkness and disclose the motives of men's hearts" (1 Corinthians 4:5). Justice can only triumph if the participants see injustices addressed and resolved. The judgment seat of Christ will be the place where God will satisfy our craving to have masks torn away, lies exposed, and reality prevail. The wrongdoers will finally admit the truth, and the victims will be vindicated; forgiveness among believers will be both given and accepted. Only then will justice prevail.

Recently I was told that a known Christian leader is actually a fake, a man who is using gullible Christians to garner funds for himself and his family. Yet he preaches messages that have biblical content; he is generally believed to have been converted out of an atheistic family. Perhaps people have been converted from hearing him preach. Whether he will be judged at the *Bema* or the Great White Throne, we can take comfort in the fact that someday the facade will fall and all that will be left is reality.

What would it be like to "suffer loss"? What would the consequences be if we did see our deeds disintegrate behind a cloud of smoke? What memories might we take with us into eternity? Notice the contrast between the two men. "If any man's work which he has built upon it remains, he shall receive a reward. If any man's work is burned up, he shall suffer loss; but he himself shall be saved, yet so as through fire" (1 Corinthians 3:14–15). The man who suffers loss is pictured as running out of a building that is engulfed in flames and collapsing behind him. He is saved; indeed, he arrives in heaven just as surely as his faithful brothers and sisters. But he has lost the opportunity for a full reward.

## LOSING OUR REWARD

What kind of lifestyle might cause us to *lose* our inheritance? We can lose our reward both by the sins we commit and the opportunities we squander. Certainly all believers inherit heaven with its opportunity to serve Christ and worship at the throne. But there is another inheritance, a special reward given to the faithful. This second kind of reward is sometimes spoken of as "inheriting eternal life."

Earlier I pointed out that some scholars teach that to *enter* the kingdom is one thing; to *inherit* the kingdom, quite another. We say that King Hussein inherited the kingdom of Jordan, which he has ruled for many years. But there are many other people who live within the country but are not participating in his rule.

To *possess* eternal life you simply need faith in Christ; to truly *inherit* it, you need faith and obedience.[4] If we keep in mind that to "inherit eternal life," or to "inherit" the kingdom, is an extra reward for faithful service, we will read many passages of Scripture differently.

Paul wrote, "For this you know with certainty, that no immoral or impure person or covetous man, who is an idolater, has an inheritance in the kingdom of Christ and God" (Ephesians 5:5). Who are these people who will not have an "inheritance in the kingdom of Christ and God"? In context, Paul is warning Christians about their behavior. He assumes that Christians can be deceived and live like the "sons of disobedience." We have all known Christians who struggle with sexual addictions, or Christians who are greedy and idolatrous. We've all known Christians who live with these sins even when coming under God's heavy hand of discipline. The Bible assumes what we know by experience, namely, that Christians can do evil deeds and be caught in terrible sins. Some die in such a spiritual condition.

Covetousness, which is also listed as one of these transgressions, lies deeply buried within every one of us. We all can identify with the war for ownership that rages within the soul. If with Christ's help we do not master such sins, they will assuredly master us. If Paul meant that those who practice such vices will not *enter* the kingdom, our own assurance of final salvation would be in constant jeopardy. Any one of us could be overtaken by such a sin and die in disgrace.

Perhaps what Paul meant is this: Those who practice such sins will not be barred from entering the kingdom, but will be barred from inheriting it. If one or more of these sins characterizes their Christian lives, and they refuse to judge the evil, they will forfeit the honor of kingdom rule.

Similar teaching occurs in Paul's instructions to the church in Galatia. In fact, here the list of sins that will prevent people from "inheriting the kingdom of God" is even longer.

> Now the deeds of the flesh are evident, which are: immorality, impurity, sensuality, idolatry, sorcery, enmities, strife, jealousy, outbursts of anger, disputes, dissensions, factions, envying, drunkenness, carousing, and things like these, *of which I forewarn you just as I have forewarned you that those who practice such things shall not inherit the kingdom of God.* (Galatians 5:19–21, italics added)

Again Paul speaks of those who will forfeit certain kingdom privileges because of their sinful lifestyle. Although we must admit that many so-called carnal Christians are not Christians at all, we also must recognize that serious failure is possible for genuine Christians. And this will be revealed at the *Bema*.[5]

I freely admit that most scholars disagree with the above interpretation. They teach that Paul's description refers to the unconverted, who will miss the *Bema* entirely and be judged at the Great White Throne Judgment. To live a lifestyle characterized by these sins, it is said, is proof that one is not a Christian. They would argue that Christians might *lapse* into these sins, but their lives will not be *characterized* by them.

It is not my intention to settle this interpretive question. Either way, Paul's words are a sober warning to all of us. First, we must examine whether we are living lives that are free of these sins which God so strictly judges. Surely many who claim to be believers and yet practice these sins are self-deceived. We must remind ourselves that it is possible to *profess* to have eternal life, and not *possess* it. In other words, many whose lives are characterized by these sins will find themselves on the wrong side of the celestial gates.

But second, I'm sure we would agree that when genuine Christians allow such sins to become a part of their lives, their reward will be diminished. Faithfulness not only means that we are committed to good deeds, but also that we are free of evil ones. One result of the new birth is a love for God and a dislike for sin. If as a child of God we tolerate what our Father hates, we will incur His discipline in this life and the next.

If we ask the question how God evaluates lives that are so mixed with failures and successes, if we wonder how God balances twenty years of faithful ministry with a year of moral failure, we cannot answer. If God spelled out specifically what we must do to "inherit" the kingdom and the number of failures that we must have on our record before we "forfeit" it, you can be sure that some of us would want to do the bare minimum to balance the ledger!

Certainly, those whose lives were characterized by these sins shall suffer greater loss than those who struggled with such sins but continually judged them through confession and repentance. Indeed, even if the sins we have forsaken and confessed will only be represented as lost rewards, they shall still greatly affect the outcome of our judgment. If we have wasted our lives, we will still suffer loss even if we should repent just before our death.

When the church at Corinth was experiencing God's heavy hand of discipline for disrespect at the Lord's Table (indeed, some were smitten with sickness and others had actually died), Paul had this admonition: "But if we judged ourselves rightly, we should not be judged. But when we are judged, we are disciplined by the Lord in order that we may not be condemned along with the world" (1 Corinthians 11:31–32).

The more consistently we judge our sins through repentance and yieldedness, the less severe will be our future judgment. Even if we should lapse into known sin, we must never make our peace with it. Unjudged sin, that is, sin that we presumptively commit, can, I believe, bar us from enjoying the full potential of our rule with Christ.

Don Carson, professor at Trinity International University, says that when he was in Europe he spoke to a student who was cheating on his wife while far away from home at a university in Germany. When Carson pointed out that this would incur the discipline of God, the adulterer responded, "Well, of course, I expect God to forgive me—that's His job!" Carson did not believe that this man was a Christian, but if a believer were to adopt such an attitude, he most assuredly would be reprimanded and denied a reward.

In the Scriptures there are many warnings to those who would misuse the grace of God. There are also many encouragements to those who strive against sin but at times lose the battle. The desires of our hearts and the direction of our lives will all be taken into account when we stand before Christ.

Keep in mind that our entire life will be evaluated. The times of spiritual victory will be assessed along with our failures. Because God is generous, He will find more good in our lives than we know is there. Remember, Paul assured us that in that day "each man's praise will come to him from God" (1 Corinthians 4:5).

A second way we can forfeit our inheritance is by refusing to accept the joys of sacrifice and single-minded devotion to Christ. Rewards are based on our consistent faithfulness to follow Christ, even at great cost. God gives each of us time, talents, and treasure. To squander these, living as though these gifts are ours and not His, is to risk forfeiting our right to rewards.

In the next chapter we will consider more specifically what Christ will be looking for when He judges us. We will list ways in which we can please or displease Him. Not everyone need leave father and mother; not everyone need suffer persecution to have an abundant entrance into the kingdom. But if we neglect our duties we will answer for our negligence.

## A MAN WHO SUFFERED LOSS

We all struggle with the concept of negative consequences at the judgment seat of Christ. Many Christians think that Christ would never reprimand us at the *Bema*. Our sins have been washed away, and God cannot judge us for our carnality, selfishness, and wasted lives, we think. Because we are not under condemnation, we feel secure that any loss we suffer cannot be too serious.

But, as we have learned, God does judge His people on earth even though they are forgiven and justified.

Ananias and Sapphira were judged by death for their dishonesty; carnal believers in Corinth died because of their disrespect for the Lord's Table (1 Corinthians 11:30). The simple principle is that God does not let His children get by with disobedience even though their place in heaven is secured and their transgressions legally forgiven. He judges them even though they will not have the opportunity to do better next time.

I agree with Kendall, who says, "We must deduce that there is no contradiction between Paul's doctrine of justification and his conception of the judgment of God; and that being declared righteous so as to escape the wrath of God . . . does not exempt us from rewards and punishment in the Last Day."[6] Thanks to Christ's sacrifice for us, we are spared the eternal penalty for our sin; we will, however, be judged for our response to opportunities that were laid before us. I can't lose my salvation, but there is something I *can* lose!

Let us try to imagine what the judgment seat of Christ will actually be like. If only we could meet someone who experienced it! The closest we can come to a firsthand account is to recall a parable Christ told about a man who suffered loss—significant loss—though he apparently was "saved . . . so as through fire" (1 Corinthians 3:15).

A nobleman called his servants and gave each of them some money and then left on his journey. One was given five talents; another, two; and a third, just one. Two of the servants seized the opportunity. "Immediately the one who had received the five talents went and traded with them, and gained five more talents. In the same manner the one who had received the two talents gained two more" (Matthew 25:16–17).

When the master returned, he called his servants to give an account of his money. When the five-talent servant presented him with ten talents, the master commended him. "Well done, good and faithful slave; you were faithful with a few things, I will put you in charge of many things, enter into the joy of your master" (v. 21). The servant whose two talents were now four talents heard the same kind words.

This corresponds to life as we know it. We are not given the same number of talents in life; some are given one, others are given two, while a few are given five or ten. God does not expect five-talent ability from a two-talent man. But since rewards are based on faithfulness to opportunity, both the two-talent man and the five-talent man received the same reward.

The third servant had hidden his money in the ground where no thief could find it. Perhaps he expected to be awarded for prudence, but he surely was not prepared for the response that awaited him. "You wicked, lazy slave, you knew that I reap where I did not sow, and gather where I scattered no seed. Then you ought to have put my money in the bank, and on my arrival I would have received my money back with interest" (vv. 26–27).

Then he added, "'Therefore take away the talent from him, and give it to the one who has the ten talents.' For to everyone who has shall more be given, and he shall have an abundance; but from the one who does not have, even what he does have shall be taken away" (vv. 28–29).

Wicked! Lazy!

The master's words stung. What had this servant done to receive such harsh condemnation? Apparently feeling inferior because he had compared himself to those who had more talents than he, he said, in effect, "If I can't have five talents, I won't use the one I do have!" If he couldn't be a five-talent man, he didn't want to be a one-talent man. The sin of comparison crippled him.

This servant also feared failure and lacked the motivation to overcome his fears. This was not just pessimism about the economy; he had made a willful decision to choose the easy path. He didn't want to take the risk of investment. He thought that a box in the dirt would be safer than an investment at the bank.

He was discontented with his talent, and so he was discontented with his God. God was cruel and powerful, reaping where He had not sown and gathering where He had not scattered. He was making unreasonable demands. I believe the servant was a bitter man because he felt cheated. He thought he was digging a hole for his talent, but actually he was digging a hole for himself. But God wasn't buying his excuses!

What did he lose?

First, *he lost the approval of his master.* "You wicked, lazy slave" (v. 26). Perhaps Christ will speak similar words to some of us in the day of judgment. These words are, after all, an expression of disappointment and grief. If we have been unfaithful, we shall be rebuked.

Second, the servant faced *temporary rejection.* "Take away the talent from him, and give it to the one who has the ten talents" (v. 28). Perhaps this helps us understand Paul's words:

> It is a trustworthy statement:
> For if we died with Him, we shall also live with Him;
> If we endure, we shall also reign with Him;

If we deny Him, He also will deny us;
If we are faithless, He remains faithful; For He cannot
    deny Himself.

(2 Timothy 2:11–13)

Paul seems to be saying that it is possible that we will not endure, in which case we might not reign with Him; it is also possible that we can deny Him, in which case He will deny us. If so, we can rejoice that even if we are faithless He will remain faithful. He will not reject us as one of His children, but as one of His servants.

Or consider the words of Christ: "For whoever is ashamed of Me and My words in this adulterous and sinful generation, the Son of Man will also be ashamed of him when He comes in the glory of His Father with the holy angels" (Mark 8:38). Imagine Christ temporarily being ashamed of us because we were ashamed of Him!

Again, I must point out that many interpreters would refer these passages of Scripture to the unconverted. No believer, it is argued, would ever permanently deny Christ; nor would any believer be consistently ashamed of Christ. Yet, in context, these warnings are addressed to believers. Paul said that if "we" deny Him, He will also deny "us." Apparently he thought that such failure was a possibility for him.

Third, the servant was *denied rule in the kingdom.* "'Therefore take away the talent from him, and give it to the one who has the ten talents.' For to everyone who has shall more be given, and he shall have an abundance; but from the one who does not have, even what he does have shall be taken away" (vv. 28–29). In a similar parable in Luke, the unfaithful servant explicitly forfeited rule over the cities (Luke 19:11–27).

In the passage in Matthew, the text records that he was cast into "outer darkness; in that place there shall be weeping and gnashing of teeth" (v. 30).

It is difficult to know how the judgment of this servant should be interpreted. Some scholars think that his strict judgment proves he was an unbeliever and perhaps Christ intended that we understand the parable as a warning to those who pretend to believe but their lifestyle belies their profession.

However, Warren Wiersbe represents those interpreters who point out that we need not see this treatment as punishment in hell, but rather the deep remorse of a man who was an unfaithful servant. He grieves deeply in the darkness outside of the King's palace, but he is still a servant and thus will be welcomed back into the King's estate. Wiersbe writes, "The man was dealt with by the Lord, he lost his opportunity for service, and he gained no praise or reward. To me that is outer darkness."[7]

We must caution that we should not build our theology on parables but remember that they were told to illustrate a central point. Christ used this story to alert His disciples to the danger of squandered opportunities. There is warning for all of us who are tempted to hide our talent in the dirt, either because of fear or self-centeredness. And when we stand before Christ in a state of purity with our glorified bodies, the sins we committed on earth will look more hideous than we could ever have thought them to be. Grief, *deep* grief, is understandable.

Can we say that some believers will be *punished* at the judgment seat of Christ? Certainly our eternal punishment was borne by Christ; thus, we are not under condemnation by God. But is not God's severe discipline of His children on earth a form of punishment?

Would not the rebuke of Christ and the loss of rewards be a form of punishment for lives carelessly lived in the face of marvelous opportunities? Is not the purpose of any judge to hand out rewards or punishment?

Let us at least boldly affirm that the negative consequences of the judgment are far-reaching. This is a judgment, an accounting of how our lives were lived, with appropriate rewards either given or withheld. In fact, we do not know whether it is even possible to recover from our showing at the *Bema*. Perhaps those who suffer loss shall miss some opportunities for all of eternity. Hoyt wisely keeps us balanced when he writes, "To overdo the sorrow aspect of the judgment seat of Christ is to make heaven into hell. To underdo the sorrow aspect is to make faithfulness inconsequential."[8]

We should not think that the unfaithful Christian will spend eternity in the outskirts of God's kingdom, cowering in a dark corner. Heaven will not be comprised of two great companies, the faithful and the unfaithful. Most of us will fall somewhere in between; and, of course, everyone will be happy, everyone fulfilled, everyone serving. But the unfaithful Christian missed a splendid experience of receiving Christ's approval. Everyone in the kingdom will be a child of God, everyone a servant, but it appears that not everyone will get to rule with Christ.

People think that as long as their ledger shows neither gain nor loss that is sufficient. No, the talent given to this servant had to earn a profit. He had to be willing to take a risk for the sake of the king and his kingdom. He had to be willing to take his jar of water and prime the pump, believing that his small investment would result in all the water he would ever need.

There is a story, a legend that comes to us from India. A beggar saw a wealthy rajah come toward him, riding in his beautiful chariot. The beggar took the opportunity and stood by the side of the road holding out his bowl of rice, hoping for a handout. To his surprise, the rajah stopped, looked at the beggar, and said, "Give me some of your rice!"

The beggar was angry. To think that this wealthy prince would expect his rice! Gingerly, he gave him one grain of rice.

"Beggar, give me more of your rice!"

In anger, the beggar gave him another grain of rice.

"More please!"

By now the beggar was seething with resentment. Once again he stingily gave the rajah another grain of rice and then walked away. As the chariot went on its way, the beggar, in his fury, looked into his bowl of rice. He noticed something glitter. It was a grain of gold, the size of a grain of rice. He looked more carefully and found just two more.

For every grain of rice, a grain of gold.

If we clutch our bowl of rice, we shall lose our reward. If we are faithful and give God each grain, He gives us gold in return.

And the gold God gives will survive the fire.

## NOTES

1. Anthony A. Hoekema, *The Bible and the Future* (Grand Rapids: Eerdmans, 1979), 259.
2. John Murray, *Lectures in Systematic Theology,* vol. 2 of *Collected Writings of John Murray* (Carlisle, Pa.: Banner of Truth, 1977), 414–15.
3. Woodrow Kroll, *Tested by Fire* (Neptune, N.J.: Loizeaux, 1977), 108.
4. Joseph C. Dillow, *The Reign of the Servant Kings* (Miami: Schoettle, 1992), 137. This detailed volume attempts to show that while the eternal destiny of believers is secure, their rewards in heaven are condi-

tioned on obedience. The author begins in the Old Testament and works through all relevant passages.

5. The question of whether "inheriting the kingdom" is the same as entering it necessitates a discussion well beyond the parameters of this book. R. T. Kendall, in *Once Saved Always Saved* (Chicago: Moody, 1983), gives extensive arguments to show that all Christians enter the kingdom but all do not "inherit it" (119–34). Joseph Dillow also adopts the same premise and labors to show that this interpretation is a more consistent understanding of the relevant texts.

6. Quoted in Dillow, 546.

7. Warren W. Wiersbe, *The Bible Exposition Commentary*, vol. 1 (Wheaton: Scripture Press, 1989), 92.

8. Quoted in Dillow, 532.

# CHAPTER FIVE

# *W*HAT CHRIST WILL BE LOOKING FOR

The more honest we are, the more tempted we will be to conclude that we will not receive any rewards. Most of us see ourselves, at least to some degree, as represented in the attitude of the unfaithful servant who buried his talent and was reprimanded by his master. As we ask God to search our hearts, we see little that is good and much that is tainted. Is there any hope that we will hear, "Well done, thou good and faithful servant"?

The thought of a thorough judgment that even exposes our hidden motives and private thoughts is more frightening than comforting. We had hoped that we could slip into heaven, sit in a back row, and not have to face our dismal performance on earth. Now that we know that everything we have thought, done, or said since our conversion will have input into the outcome, we are not sure whether we want to die to be with Christ. We hope that there will be nuggets of gold amid the wood, hay, and stubble, but they probably will be few and far between. At least that is how all honest Christians feel.

How can any one of us expect to receive anything at all? Let us honestly affirm that not a one of us has all of the works that the Bible presents as being worthy of a reward. Our opportunities are limited, our lives too short, and our hearts too sinful. Some Christians are confined to a wheelchair; or they might be in prison, where the opportunities to serve are few.

Our motives are seldom as pure as we would like them to be; if our inner lives were exposed for all to see we would want to live alone on a deserted island.

It is time for some encouragement.

First, let us keep in mind that the value of a deed depends upon the attitude of the heart. If we wanted to do more for Christ but could not because of human limitations, God will take our desires into account. We will be judged on the basis of faithfulness to the opportunities presented to us.

For example, when it comes to giving, Paul stresses the attitude of the heart. "For if the readiness is present, it is acceptable according to what a man has, not according to what he does not have" (2 Corinthians 8:12). If you give ten dollars but would give more if you had it, you will be rewarded for more than the amount you gave. If you intended to give a dollar you will be rewarded for a dollar even if you inadvertently placed a twenty-dollar bill on the plate! The widow's two mites were almost worthless when we consider the huge budget needed to finance the temple worship. Yet Christ said, "This poor widow hath cast more in, than all they which have cast into the treasury," for she "cast in all that she had, even all her living" (Mark 12:43–44, KJV). Her gift was especially precious because she gave from her heart, unaware that Christ was watching. Her generous character counted.

We should notice in passing that a good motive does not mean that we enjoy doing a particular deed. Surely the slaves in Paul's time did not delight in treating their masters (often cruel) as they would treat Christ. God often asks us to do hard things, to suffer unjustly, and to endure suffering of every sort. The test of a motive is whether it is done for Christ, quite apart from whether the experience was pleasant or not.

Second, keep in mind that Christ takes our deeds, if done in His name, and makes them acceptable to the Father. Truth is, even when we serve with a motive that is as selfless as humanly possible, our deeds are still tainted with sin. We help a woman across a street, but often it is to make ourselves feel good because we all want to be needed. And perhaps that evening we can tell our family that we did our good deed for the day. We give money to the work of the church and secretly hope that the word will get out that we are among the generous.

One day a young woman abandoned her car and was walking along the street in obvious distress. I stopped and learned that her car had run out of gas. So I drove to a gas station, purchased a can filled with gas, and drove back to her car. As I was pouring gas into her car while standing in the ditch dressed in my business suit, the thought came to me, *I wish that all the people of Moody Church could see me now!*

Mixed motives.

How can these works become acceptable to God? Can we be rewarded for deeds done with motives that are not entirely loving, free of all self-interest? Yes, here again our Savior prepares us for the day when He will be our judge. We are not to work for Christ as an employee for an employer; we are to work for Him as sons and daughters within a loving family. *Christ works in us and for us to please the Father!*

Christ takes our acts done with our good intentions and cleanses them so that they might be acceptable to God. Peter wrote, "You also, as living stones, are being built up as a spiritual house for a holy priesthood, to offer up spiritual sacrifices acceptable to God through Jesus Christ" (1 Peter 2:5). *Sacrifices acceptable through Christ!*

We've learned that good deeds done before our conversion are of no merit whatsoever; but the reason that good deeds after our conversion have merit is because they are presented to the Father through Christ! Because we are joined to Christ, we might say that He sees Christ as having done them!

Paul said that we should approve the things that are excellent "in order to be sincere and blameless until the day of Christ; having been filled with the fruit of righteousness which comes through Jesus Christ, to the glory and praise of God" (Philippians 1:10b–11). Through Jesus Christ our deeds of righteousness are "to the glory and praise of God." The Reformers were right: Before our salvation our deeds have no merit whatever in God's sight. But they should also have stressed that after our conversion we can present ourselves to God, and this offering becomes "a living and holy sacrifice, acceptable to God, which is your spiritual service of worship" (Romans 12:1b).

God is especially pleased when He sees His Son in us. Thus after our conversion, our deeds should no longer originate in the flesh but in the work of the Spirit. Christ taught, "Abide in Me, and I in you. As the branch cannot bear fruit of itself, unless it abides in the vine, so neither can you, unless you abide in Me.

. . . for apart from Me you can do nothing" (John 15:4–5). Obviously, apart from Christ we can do many things; but we can do nothing that will last.

Christ calls us to bear fruit that endures. Although fruit perishes quickly, there is a kind of fruit that will last forever. This is the fruit of the Spirit, the supernatural work of the Holy Spirit in our lives. *The works that are most acceptable are those done with the conviction that there is no merit in us but in Christ.*

The good deeds Christ will be looking for have common characteristics: a willingness to sacrifice, a joyous faith, and a commitment to persevere as did Moses. "And without faith it is impossible to please Him, for he who comes to God must believe that He is, and that He is a rewarder of those who seek Him" (Hebrews 11:6). And, of course, at the root is a love for God, a willingness to serve, knowing that whatever the Father gives us is good for us. Yes, it is true that *God looks for the works that He Himself has wrought in us!*

Here are the deeds that are especially highlighted, the deeds that bring the promise of "great reward" (Hebrews 10:35).

## WHAT CHRIST IS LOOKING FOR

### The Joyful Acceptance of Injustice

Christ was straightforward about the reward connected with bearing insults for His sake. "Blessed are you when men cast insults at you, and persecute you, and say all kinds of evil against you falsely, on account of Me. Rejoice, and be glad, for your reward in heaven is great, for so they persecuted the prophets who were before you" (Matthew 5:11–12). If you are fired from a job because of your faith in Christ, if you are ostracized from the company perks, if you are bypassed in the pay scale because your convictions will not allow you to be dishonest—rejoice, for your reward is great in heaven!

A doctor friend of mine says that he is considered a troublemaker because he keeps calling his hospital administration to embrace integrity. Even fellow Christians think he should not rock the boat because everyone is affected. But he is a Christian with clear convictions, and he cannot be satisfied until he has done what he can to get the hospital to own up to its procedures and practices.

The author of Hebrews warned his readers that if they did not suffer for Christ successfully, they would be losers. "Therefore, do not throw away your confidence, which has a great reward" (10:35). The deep conviction that God was testing them in their distress would give them the courage to remain loyal even though their property was being seized and they were being ostracized for their faith. The knowledge of a "great reward" would give them the motivation they needed.

Peter wrote, "For this finds favor, if for the sake of conscience toward God a man bears up under sorrows when suffering unjustly" (1 Peter 2:19). Our cross is simply the trouble we wouldn't have if we were not Christians. Let us accept such trouble in the name of Christ and rejoice! God is watching.

## Financial Generosity

Christ repeatedly spoke about money as being a test of our loyalties. He said, in fact, that if we cannot be entrusted with the mammon of unrighteousness, we should not think that we will be given more important spiritual responsibilities. He chided the Pharisees for their love of money and then said, "For that which is highly esteemed among men is detestable in the sight of God" (Luke 16:15).

Here is His familiar promise:

> Do not lay up for yourselves treasures upon earth, where moth nor rust destroy, and where thieves break in and steal. But lay up for yourselves treasures in heaven, where neither moth nor rust destroys, and where thieves do not break in or steal; for where your treasure is, there will your heart be also. (Matthew 6:19–21)

In our churches we are very careful not to reveal how much people give; gifts are strictly confidential. There are two reasons for this. One is that we might give in secret so as to be rewarded openly. The other is that we might not be tempted to treat the large donors with greater respect. But the real reason might be because we give so little we would be embarrassed if everyone knew how much we gave. But if that which is secret will be revealed, the day is coming when our checkbook will be carefully examined.

However, it would be a mistake to think that we will be judged solely on the basis of what we gave to the church, the poor, and missions. Let us never forget that all of our money belongs to God. This means that whatever we spend to live on, whatever we invest or inherit—we shall be accountable for all of it. Blessed is the child who looks into the face of his heavenly Father and asks for wisdom to use all his resources for the glory of God. (Since the subject of money was so frequently discussed by Christ, we shall consider investment strategies in the next chapter.)

## Hospitality

Suppose Christ was scheduled to pay a visit to your church, and the pastor was looking for a home in which He could stay. Imagine the lineup of anxious Christians, all insisting that He come home with them!

Indeed someday Christ will invite people into His kingdom and say, "For I was hungry, and you gave Me something to eat; I was thirsty, and you gave Me drink; I was a stranger, and you invited Me in; naked, and you clothed Me; I was sick, and you visited Me; I was in prison, and you came to Me" (Matthew 25:35–36).

And when His people are startled because they do not remember having personally done this, Christ responds, "Truly I say to you, to the extent that you did it to one of these brothers of Mine, even the least of them, you did it to Me" (v. 40). We can sign up to have Christ visit us! We can take Him home with us any night of the week.

And what do we get in return? That depends, of course, on the attitude with which we exercised our hospitality. Christ describes the kindness that will not escape His notice.

> When you give a luncheon or a dinner, do not invite your friends or your brothers or your relatives or rich neighbors, lest they also invite you in return, and repayment come to you. But when you give a reception, invite the poor, the crippled, the lame, the blind, and you will be blessed, since they do not have the means to repay you; for you will be repaid at the resurrection of the righteous. (Luke 14:12–14)

Christ did not shy away from calling rewards "repayments." If you want to please Christ, find the poor, the physically challenged, and the lonely and throw a feast for them. You will be "repaid" in the day of resurrection.

If you are tempted to envy a prophet because your own gifts are so small in comparison, you can receive a "prophet's reward."

> He who receives you receives Me, and he who receives Me receives Him who sent Me. He who receives a prophet in the name of a prophet shall receive a prophet's reward; and he who receives a righteous man in the name of a righteous man shall receive a righteous man's reward. (Matthew 10:40–41).

Edwin Markam wrote a poem about waiting for an appointment to meet with Christ.

> ***How the Great Guest Came***
> *Why is it, Lord, that your feet delay?*
> *Did you forget this was the day?*
> *Then soft in the silence a voice he heard,*
> *Lift up your heart for I kept my word.*
> *I was the beggar with bruised feet,*
> *I was the woman you gave to eat,*
> *I was the child on the homeless street.*

With a child standing beside Him, Christ said, "And whoever receives one such child in My name receives Me" (Matthew 18:5).

## The Spiritual Disciplines

The Jews had three spiritual disciplines they habitually practiced: the giving of alms, prayer, and fasting.

Christ warned that these should not be exercised publicly to be seen of men. Indeed, those who do these things to look good "have their reward in full" (Matthew 6:5).

- "But when you give alms, do not let your left hand know what your right hand is doing that your alms may be in secret; and your Father who sees in secret will repay you" (vv. 3–4).
- "But you, when you pray, go into your inner room, and when you have shut your door, pray to your Father who is in secret, and your Father who sees in secret will repay you" (v. 6).
- "But you, when you fast, anoint your head, and wash your face so that you may not be seen fasting by men, but by your Father who is in secret; and your Father who sees in secret will repay you" (vv. 17–18).

Christ taught that it is possible to succeed in the eyes of men and fail in the eyes of God. If we serve to be seen of men, we will be rewarded by them. To quote Christ, we will "have [our] reward in full." We will not be rewarded twice. If we get all of our strokes in this life, we should expect no repayment in the life to come. *We are rewarded by the person whose praise we seek.*

In fact, when we are overlooked or taken for granted, and when the credit for what we do goes to someone else, we can rejoice, for God will give us a greater reward. Secret deeds often have purer motives than public ones. Blessed are those who have many secrets with God.

Of course, we will be judged not only by whether we practiced the disciplines of the Christian life. We will also be held accountable for the way in which we lived the whole of life. All of our time, talent, and treasure belongs to God.

## Faithfulness in Our Vocation

The painful fact is that many people simply never find the right job/gift mix. Multitudes—perhaps the majority of the work force—dislike what they are doing. But the need for money forces them into jobs that ignite boredom, frustration, and conflict. Many are underpaid.

Put yourself in a time machine and go back two thousand years and imagine that you are one of the 60 million slaves in the Roman Empire. You have no rights, no chance for a promotion, no court of appeals. To such, Paul wrote that they should serve their masters as they would serve Christ.

> Slaves, in all things obey those who are your masters on earth, not with external service, as those who merely please men, but with sincerity of heart, fearing the Lord. Whatever you do, do your work heartily, as for the Lord rather than for men; knowing that from the Lord you will receive the reward of the inheritance. It is the Lord Christ whom you serve. (Colossians 3:22–24)

Paul is not insensitive to their plight. He urges their masters to be fair, and he knew that the only way he could fight slavery in those days was by preaching the gospel. This would transform both slave and master so that there might be mutual respect and fairness. But even in the absence of such circumstances, Paul could exhort slaves to serve their masters as if serving

Christ because they would be recompensed by Him. The Lord will make up for the wages they didn't receive and the mistreatment they endured—and then some!

In the world, greatness is determined by the number of people you rule; power is the name of the game. In the kingdom, greatness is determined by the number of people you serve. Humility is the badge of highest honor. Indeed, Christ Himself was exalted because He came not to be served, but to serve and give His life for us. "He humbled Himself by becoming obedient to the point of death, even death on a cross. *Therefore* also God highly exalted Him" (Philippians 2:8–9, italics added).

Ironically, if you want to have the possibility of ruling at Christ's right hand, don't seek it by trying to find a lofty position and use it as a stepping-stone to something greater. Find the most lowly position, and perhaps God will grant you an exalted position. "Humble yourselves, therefore, under the mighty hand of God, that He may exalt you at the proper time" (1 Peter 5:6).

Blessed are those who change masters without changing jobs! If we visualize receiving our paychecks from Christ and not our employer, we will view our work very differently. And someday we will be generously compensated. God will not only judge you for how you taught your Sunday school class but for how you did your job on Monday morning.

Servanthood, as we shall learn in a future chapter, is the stepping-stone to greatness. Even better, servanthood *is* greatness.

## Loving the Unlovable

Christ taught that there was a difference between divine love and human love. Human love depends upon the one who is loved. If you meet my needs, if I find you attractive, and if our personalities are compatible, I will love you. Understandably, human love changes. "You're not the woman I married!" a man shouts, giving his rationale for a divorce.

In contrast, divine love depends upon the lover; divine love says I can go on loving you even if you have stopped loving me. Divine love is based on a decision that continues even if the one who is loved changes. Divine love says, "You cannot make me stop loving you."

In this context, read Christ's words: "But I say to you who hear, love your enemies, do good to those who hate you, bless those who curse you, pray for those who mistreat you" (Luke 6:27–28). This kind of love even loves enemies. And if we want to know whether such tough love will really be worth the cost, Christ continues, "But love your enemies, and do good, and lend, expecting nothing in return; and your reward will be great, and you will be sons of the Most High; for He Himself is kind to ungrateful and evil men" (v. 35). *Your reward will be great!*

So often we pray, "O God, make me godly." We want to be like God. Then God sends a difficult person into our life—perhaps a quarrelsome co-worker—and we complain, insisting that He remove the "thorn" from us. But these trials are given to us that we might become "godly."

You have it from Christ Himself. "Your reward shall be great!"

## Doctrinal Integrity

In a letter written by the apostle John to a church that evidently was known as "the chosen lady" (2 John 1), he warned the believers that there were many false teachers who could do a great deal of damage within the assembly. There were, he said, many deceivers, who denied that Jesus Christ has come in the flesh. They were, in effect, antichrists.

The believers were to watch out for the disastrous spiritual effects that might result from any compromise with their ideas. If they did not do so, they might lose some of their reward. "Watch yourselves, that you might not lose what we have accomplished, but that you may receive a full reward" (v. 8). Notice that if they did fail, they might not lose their entire reward, but would lose their "full reward."

Certainly those who refuse to guard the doctrine of the faith are liable to discipline and loss of reward. Sound doctrine, on the other hand, will merit a more complete reward in the day of judgment.

## Investment in People

Only people span the gap between time and eternity. Paul writes: "For who is our hope or joy or crown of exultation? Is it not even you, in the presence of our Lord Jesus at His coming?" (1 Thessalonians 2:19). God's people are His most highly prized possession. To love those who are His, to invest in their spiritual well-being, is to attract special consideration. Exercising our gifts for the benefit of the body merits eternal reward.

Our investment in the lives of others varies in accordance with our gifts and opportunities. Some will sow, others water, still others reap; yet each shall be properly rewarded. These words, quoted before, deserve to be repeated:

I planted, Apollos watered, but God gave the increase. So then neither he who plants is anything, nor
he who waters, but God who gives the increase. Now
he who plants and he who waters are one, and each
one will receive his own reward according to his own
labor. (1 Corinthians 3:6–8, NKJV)

Please do not overlook the last line: "Each one will
receive his own reward according to his own labor."
There is a specific connection between the opportunities I accept and the rewards I receive.

## Watching for Christ's Return

Christ has always insisted that wise servants look
out for their master's arrival. He says:

Be dressed in readiness, and keep your lamps alight.
And be like men who are waiting for their master
when he returns from the wedding feast, so that they
may immediately open the door to him when he comes
and knocks. Blessed are those slaves whom the master shall find on the alert when he comes; truly I say
to you, that he will gird himself to serve, and have
them recline at the table, and will come up and wait
on them. Whether he comes in the second watch, or
even in the third, and finds them so, blessed are those
slaves. (Luke 12:35–38)

We admire the apostle Paul for his endurance in
preaching the gospel. We wish we had his revelations
and opportunities. Yet we have the opportunity to be
rewarded just as he was. When he was about to die,
he looked back and could say: "I have fought the
good fight, I have finished the course, I have kept the

faith" (2 Timothy 4:7). He expected to receive "the crown of righteousness, which the Lord, the righteous Judge, will award to me on that day; and not only to me, but also to all who have loved His appearing" (v. 8).

Whatever interpretation we give to the "crown of righteousness," we can have it too! To love the appearing of Christ is to receive a special welcome into heaven.

When soloist George Beverley Shea was asked what he would like to be when Christ returned, he said, "On pitch!" Let us all be ready to praise the Lamb when He returns.

## Acceptance of Suffering

While speaking on the West Coast, I met a man whose wife had a rare, debilitating disease. He had to give her constant care, for she was confined to a wheelchair. Worse than the physical limitations, however, were her mental and emotional states of anger and continual discontent. If they went to church, she might appear pleasant, but on the way home she would berate him for everything from his own conversations with people to his driving. "I receive no thanks, no kind words, no sense of teamwork," he told me.

I was so moved by his story that I told him, "I don't expect to see you in heaven!" He was shocked, of course, but then I continued. "You will be so close to the throne, and I will be so far back, I will not see you!" And I meant every word. There are some people whom God calls to a special kind of suffering. Their faithfulness is of great reward.

When Christ returns, all of us would like to have something to present to Him. Peter wrote, "That the proof of your faith, being more precious than gold which is perishable, even though tested by fire, may be found to result in praise and glory and honor at the revelation of Jesus Christ" (1 Peter 1:7). Trials are given to us that we might be able to develop the faith that is precious to Christ. This faith, although a gift of God to us, nevertheless will be found to the praise and honor of Christ.

Of course, if I am faithful, I will have the same opportunity to be "close to the throne," as I put it. Furthermore, there are many ways to receive rewards. We've already listed more deeds than any one of us could consistently do. We will not be chided for the deeds we could not perform, though we undoubtedly will be shown what our lives could have been like had we lived them faithfully for Christ. We can rejoice: "For God is not unjust so as to forget your work and the love which you have shown toward His name, in having ministered and in still ministering to the saints" (Hebrews 6:10).

We do not know everything we would like to know about rewards. We simply do not understand how Christ will balance our good deeds with those that are worthless. We must be content to know that Christ will be fair and generous. Whatever He does will be acceptable; no one will question His judgment. He will meticulously separate the perishable from the imperishable.

Upon hearing of the assassination of John and Betty Stamm in China in 1934, Will Houghton, former president of Moody Bible Institute, wrote these words:

> So this is life. This world with its pleasures, struggles and tears, a smile, a frown, a sigh, friendship so true and love of kin and neighbor? Sometimes it is hard to live—always to die!
>
> The world moves on so rapidly for the living; the forms of those who disappear are replaced, and each

one dreams that he will be enduring. How soon that one becomes the missing face!

Help me to know the value of these hours. Help me the folly of all waste to see. Help me to trust the Christ who bore my sorrows and thus to yield for life or death to Thee.

If we could catch a glimpse of heaven, we would strain to make the best use of the opportunities presented to us. Our lives, said James, are "just a vapor that appears for a little while and then vanishes away" (4:14). There is much that awaits us on the other side.

And now we turn to the one matter Christ referred to repeatedly, a sensitive subject that gives us the potential of great failure or great reward.

Don't stop now.

# CHAPTER SIX

# ᏀAKING IT WITH YOU

Y ou can "beat the system"!

Perhaps you heard of the employer who fired his branch manager for squandering money. The manager was humiliated and at a loss as to how he might earn a living. Physically, he was not strong enough to do hard labor and he was too filled with pride to beg for food. He did not know anyone who would give him a job that would be in keeping with his aptitudes and desires.

An idea struck him. If he got busy and made some friends, they might give him a job or at least a place to stay for the next few weeks. If he talked money, they would listen.

Before he cleaned out his desk he called some of his master's clients and made a proposal. He would re-negotiate their contracts so that they did not have to pay the boss all they owed. For example, if they owed a hundred bushels of wheat, he cut the amount to fifty;

the man who owed a barrel of oil now owed only a half barrel. Needless to say, the patrons were grateful.

When his boss discovered this bit of wheeling and dealing he was angry, but he did have to commend his steward for shrewdness. If he had stolen the money, he could have been sent to prison; but he didn't steal, he just "gave it away." He was smart to use money to make friends so that after he was fired he would know some people who would do him a good turn.

Perhaps you recognize this story as the one Christ told to illustrate the wise use of money. He does not commend the morals of the man (He calls him an "un-righteous steward"), but He does commend him for his cleverness. Then He adds, "For the sons of this age are more shrewd in relation to their own kind than the sons of light. And I say to you, make friends for yourselves by means of the mammon of unrighteousness; that when it fails, they may receive you into the eternal dwellings" (Luke 16:8–9).

This is not a chapter about giving, but *investing*. If we use money wisely we can "beat the system." We can "take it with us" with handsome dividends. This chapter, perhaps more than any other, will give specific instruction on how to make sure that there will be a reward waiting for us in heaven. If you are a wise investor, listen carefully.

## PRINCIPLES OF SOUND FINANCIAL MANAGEMENT

What we need is a philosophy of money, an opportunity to step back and look at it from God's point of view. When we are finished, we will never see wealth in the same way again. And we will discover that money can bridge the gap from this life to the next.

Here are five principles of sound financial management. The sooner we memorize them, the more productive we will be in this life and the greater our reward in the next.

## Money Is Loaned, Not Owned

Thousands of Christians mismanage their money because they see it through a skewed lens. They think that the money put in the offering plate is God's, but the rest is theirs to spend as they please. And because of this misunderstanding, God is not free to bless them. The steward in Christ's parable owned nothing, but he was put in charge of everything. He knew that not a dime of what he managed belonged to him. He also knew that he was being watched and would have to give an account for what he did with all that was given.

Christ states flatly that money is not ours. "And if you have not been faithful in the use of that which is another's, who will give you that which is your own?" (Luke 16:12). Our money belongs to "another." Some of our wages are already garnished for federal and state taxes before we bring our check home. Bills have to be paid; creditors remind us that some of our money is theirs. Our money is "another's."

And even if we should save some of it, we might lose it in a stock market crash, and then it will surely become another's. And if money is not taken away from us, we will be taken away from it. It never was ours to keep. God loaned it to us, and He will receive it back.

The first step to receive God's blessing is to consciously recognize His ownership over all we possess. We must make Him Lord of our bank accounts, stocks, bonds, and mutual funds. Yes, our retirement accounts too. Then we have to pray for wisdom to manage all of this according to His principles and long-range intentions.

Yes, we might keep some of these savings, but we will always look at money differently once we realize that none of it is *owned;* it is only *loaned.* Accountability is now never far from our minds.

If you have never done so before, consciously transfer your money, real estate, and other assets into the hands of God. Trust Him to give you the wisdom to use these wisely and productively. A farmer whose crop was knocked down by hail said he felt bad until he remembered whose crop it really was. God, he realized, has a right to do what He wishes with that which belongs to Him.

Better it be in His hands than ours.

## Money Should Be Transmuted into More Lasting Investments

During the Middle Ages alchemists experimented to find a chemical that would turn lead into gold. The intention was to transform common metals into something more valuable. In a different way, we do this all the time; we are always changing money into something else. This process is called *transmutation.*

For example, just yesterday one of our daughters needed a prescription filled. So I went to the bank, but I did not return home to give her money to eat; if so, she would have needed more than a prescription! I did take the money to the drug store and transmuted it into medicine; I also transmuted it into groceries and a newspaper. Transmutation means the changing across to something else.

104

If you are a smart investor, you will always be thinking of ways to transmute your money into more secure investments. When stocks are down, look for money market funds; when inflation is out of control, you might want some of your investments in precious metals. The wiser you are, the more carefully you will watch for secure returns. Christ taught that there were even better investments. We can transmute our funds to bridge the gap between earth and heaven. We can use our money to make friends who will welcome us into "eternal dwellings."

This can be done indirectly. The Christians at Philippi supported Paul in his missionary ventures, and now that he was imprisoned in Rome they sent a gift to help him. Paul wrote to thank them, but he does not say anything about what the gift meant to him, but rather what it meant to *them*. He writes, "Not that I am looking for a gift, but I am looking for what may be credited to your account" (Philippians 4:17, NIV). Giving does not help the recipient as much as it helps the giver himself, who is upping his tally in the accounts of heaven.

When we support missionaries who make converts, when we help in the lives of those who spread the gospel, we are hearing about something of ultimate value. But these values are obtained by starting on the lower level. Who pledged $1,000 for missions last year? Who decided to support that missionary couple that went to Haiti? Whoever did it learned the secret of taking something of lower value and transmuting it upward to something of higher value. That's wisdom.

There is a story told of a European princess, a fervent Christian, who was burdened to start an orphanage for street children. She did not have any money of her own, so she told her husband she wanted to sell the jewels he had given her so that she could help the orphans.

Of course he was reluctant. "Don't you appreciate the jewels?" he would ask. "Of course," she would reply. "But there are homeless children we could help."

Eventually he gave in. She sold the jewels for many thousands of dollars and was able to build the orphanage. The children came and were fed and shown love. They memorized verses of Scripture and sang songs. One day the princess returned to her husband, "I found my jewels today!" she said through tears of joy. "I found my jewels, the bright happy eyes of the children who were rescued from the streets. I found my jewels!"

Smart woman! She beat the system!

All of our lives we are told that we "cannot take it with us." We are told we have to leave it all behind. Of course, we cannot take dollars and jewels with us, but if we transmute these into heavenly values, we can meet our money in another life. The princess found a way to get her jewels on the other side of eternity; she took them all the way to heaven. Forever.

Luther would commend this woman. He said, "I have held many things in my hands, and I have lost them all. But whatever I have placed in God's hands, that I still possess." If the value of an investment is determined by its security and rate of return, investing in the lives of those who will live forever brings the best dividends. God does not want us to give so that we become poorer; rather, we are to give so that we might become richer.

Giving to God's work is like investing in a mutual fund. You are contributing to a variety of ministries, each of which will have a high rate of return in new investments that jump the gap between time and eternity, between earth and heaven. "Lay up for your-selves treasures in heaven, where neither moth nor rust destroys, and where thieves do not break in or steal" (Matthew 6:20).

Of course, we can also make such investments more directly. We can spend money to take our friends out to dinner and share the good news of the gospel with them. We can buy Bibles and books and distribute them in our community. We can welcome our neighbors into our homes.

We can also help the poor, befriend the unemployed, and take a cake to the widow across the street. If done for Christ, we will not lose our reward; it will be waiting for us in the heavenly kingdom.

## Money Is a Test for Greater Privileges

Christ turns our view of money upside down.

He says, "He who is faithful in a very little thing is faithful also in much; and he who is unrighteous in a very little thing is unrighteous also in much. If therefore you have not been faithful in the use of unrighteous mammon, who will entrust the true riches to you?" (Luke 16:10–11).

First of all He calls it "a very little thing." Now, if you know anything about the world, you know that money is a "very big thing"! Money is the lifeblood of business; it lies at the heart of "the deal." People lie for it, steal for it, scheme for it, and die for it.

A recent newspaper article titled "Not for Love but for Money" begins, "The romantic ideal of 'live now, pay later' is becoming increasingly dated in England." The report goes on to say that more people than ever now take financial security into account when sizing up a potential marriage partner. "Romance is no longer enough," the report says. "People want to marry someone with some money."

For us, money is not "a little thing."

Second, Christ calls it "unrighteous mammon." We might paraphrase it "filthy lucre." Not very complimentary, but woefully true. Just look at what people have done for money!

Haddon Robinson, whose message on this parable has impacted my own thinking, points out that Christ does not play word games like we do. We often hear it said, "There is nothing wrong with money. It's just the *love* of it that's wrong!" But, notes Robinson, we use this cliché as an excuse, a convenient cover for our covetousness. We tell ourselves we really don't *love* money. Mind you, we date it, snuggle up to it, fantasize about it, scheme about it, hoard it—but we don't *love* it!

Christ does not let us by with neat rationalizations. He calls money what it is because He knows what people have done to get it. He knows the businessman who has cheated, the prostitute who has sold her body, the family that has feuded over settling an estate. He knows how covetous we are and that "covetousness . . . is idolatry" (Colossians 3:5, KJV).

Let's not miss Christ's three contrasts.

- If we are unfaithful in a "very little thing," how can God entrust us with something greater in the world to come?
- If we fail in the responsible use of the "the mammon of unrighteousness," how can we be counted worthy of the greater riches in the kingdom?
- If we misuse "that which is another's," how can the Lord entrust us with the inheritance He desires to give us?

Money is a test to see whether we are worthy to rule with Christ, able to assume full responsibilities in His reign and glory. Those who have the wisdom to transmute their funds into more permanent treasures are wise indeed. Consider: Many of us have money deducted from our paychecks to help fatten our retirement accounts. This might be prudent, considering the fact that we will probably live well beyond the days of our earning power. But think how irresponsible we are if we do not similarly have money set aside regularly to specifically advance the kingdom so that we might have many friends who welcome us into "eternal dwellings"!

I've known Christians who put a twenty-dollar bill in the offering plate if they just happen to have that much in their wallet. They do not have a giving plan that resembles their saving plan. They do not give as much as they can and then wish they could give more. They are unfaithful, and their status in heaven will reflect it.

If we cannot be trusted to wisely administer God's money on earth, what makes us think we will be capable stewards in heaven? Greed here on earth means we forfeit the right to enter into all that could be ours in heaven. And what we don't use, we will lose, just as the unfaithful servant discovered when the king returned.

Money is our trust. God is testing us to see whether we are prepared for the larger responsibilities that await the faithful.

## Money Must Be Our Servant or It Will Be Our Master

Christ ended this parable by saying, "No servant can serve two masters; for either he will hate the one, and love the other, or else he will hold to one, and despise the other. You cannot serve God and mammon" (Luke 16:13).

We cannot be a full-time slave to two masters. If we serve God with our whole heart, the seductive love of money will be squeezed out. We must fight to make money our servant, asking God to root its power out of our lives. Even then, it will seek to grow again, for money is seductive and deceitful. We must agree with John Wesley, who said, "I value all things only by the price they shall gain in eternity."

Our hearts cannot have two ultimate loyalties.

## Money Must Be Transmuted for Heaven or Lost Forever

The Pharisees to whom Christ told this parable were livid. They did not buy into this "use your money for people who will be in heaven" message. We read, "Now the Pharisees, who were lovers of money, were listening to all these things, and they were scoffing at Him" (Luke16:14). No lover of money likes what Christ had to say.

In order to convince them that money would not help them once they died, Christ told a story about a rich man who was "habitually dressed in purple and fine linen, gaily living in splendor every day. And a certain poor man named Lazarus was laid at his gate, covered with sores" (vv. 19–20). Incredibly, in the life to come their fortunes were reversed! Lazarus was carried by angels into Abraham's bosom; the rich man was delivered to hades, where he languished in darkness, isolation, and torment. Lazarus, who endured so much ill treatment when he was living, was now comforted; the rich man was in agony.

Christ's point is not that we are saved by being poor. He means to teach us that riches will not help us when we die. We cannot use them to hire an attorney to plead our case; we cannot use them to build ourselves a home or purchase some creature comforts. To the Pharisees who loved money, Christ was saying, "Riches are deceptive! They cannot provide what you really need!" Only those who consciously transfer their funds to heaven understand true values.

## THE DAY YOUR DOLLARS DIE

Germany lay in ruins.

Millions of refugees wandered the streets in German cities amid the rubble of bombed-out buildings and disheveled streets. Years would be necessary to rebuild. The memory of Adolph Hitler would never be forgotten.

Willard Cantelon, in his book *The Day the Dollar Dies,* recounts the story of a little German mother who wanted to assist the building of a Bible school on the outskirts of the destroyed city of Frankfurt. She held her money with pride and tenderness, as though it was a part of her very life. She had earned this money with hard work and had constantly guarded it in the war's destructive years. Now "she was investing it in a worthy cause and beamed with pride as she offered her contribution."

Cantelon continues, "How could I tell her she had held this money too long? Why did it fall my lot to shock this sensitive soul with the news that her money was virtually worthless? Why had she not read the morning paper, or heard the announcement that the new government in Bonn had cancelled this currency?"[1]

That Sunday in June of 1948, a staggering number of Germans committed suicide. Millions lost their savings because the mark had been canceled by their government. If only they had exchanged their money for something that would survive the economic collapse!

If this dear lady—bless her—had brought her money sooner, those marks could have helped pay for the renovation of the facilities or the tuition of students. Too bad that she had to hear those disappointing words, "Madam, I'm awfully sorry, but I cannot accept your money."

Someday, every dollar, every piece of gold, and every jewel will be devalued, wiped out forever. Peter wrote: "But the day of the Lord will come like a thief, in which the heavens will pass away with a roar and the elements will be destroyed with intense heat, and the earth and its works will be burned up" (2 Peter 3:10).

So much for Wall Street. Good-bye to stocks, bonds, property, and gold. Good-bye to houses, condos, and cars. The wise investor will put his money in a place that will bring the greatest dividends for the longest time. We cannot take dollars and Krugerrands with us unless we transmute them into something that will bridge the gap between earth and heaven.

On a wall in a New York rescue mission there are these lines:

*Angels from their realms on High*
*Look down on us with wondrous eye*
*That where we are but passing guests*
*We build such strong and solid nests*
*But where we hope to dwell for aye*
*We scarce take heed one stone to lay.*

The stones we lay on the other side will help determine whether we are worthy to reign in the kingdom. If we are faithful in "the little thing," we will be faithful over the true riches. We will join those who reign over greater treasures.

The wise take it with them.

## NOTE

1. Willard Cantelon, *The Day the Dollar Dies: Biblical Prophecy of a New World System in the End Times* (Plainfield, N.J.: Logos International, 1973), vi–vii.

# CHAPTER SEVEN

# ℛUN TO WIN

There is a story about a frustrated basketball coach, Cotton Fitzsimmons, who hit on an idea to motivate his team. Before the game he gave them a speech that centered around the word *pretend*. "Gentlemen, when you go out there tonight, instead of remembering that we are in last place, pretend we are in first place; instead of being in a losing streak, pretend we are in a winning streak; instead of this being a regular game, pretend this is a play-off game!"

With that, the team went onto the basketball court and were soundly beaten by the Boston Celtics. Coach Fitzsimmons was upset about the loss. But one of the players slapped him on the back and said, "Cheer up, Coach! *Pretend* we won!"

Many of us appear to be winning in the race of life, but perhaps it is all "pretend." Standing before Christ we will soon see the difference between an actual victory and wishful thinking. We will see what it took to win and what it took to lose. We'll discover that we were playing for keeps.

Paul loved to use athletic contests as an analogy for living the Christian life. The famous Greek marathon and the Isthmian Games in Corinth were a ready illustration of how to run the race that really counts. We are running the race, Paul taught, and we are running to win.

> Do you not know that those who run in a race all run, but only one receives the prize? Run in such a way that you may win. And everyone who competes in the games exercises self-control in all things. They then do it to receive a perishable wreath, but we an imperishable. Therefore I run in such a way, as not without aim; I box in such a way, as not beating the air; but I buffet my body and make it my slave, lest possibly, after I have preached to others, I myself should be disqualified. (1 Corinthians 9:24–27)

Let's not miss Paul's point: *Whatever makes a winning athlete will make a winning Christian.* If we were as committed in our walk with God as we are to golf or bowling, we will do well in the Christian life. We can take what we learn in our tennis lessons and apply it to Christian living. Think of the energy, time, and money spent on sports. If we would transfer such resources to the race that really counts, we would all be winners.

Society does not develop saints. There is nothing in our culture that will encourage us to have the stamina and encouragement to become winners for Christ. Indeed, we shall have to buck the world at every turn of the road; we shall have to rely on God and His people to help us develop the disciplines that lead to godliness.

Let's introduce the analogy.

In Greece you had to be a citizen in order to compete in the games. Of course, all citizens were not in the races, but if you were eligible, you had to give proof of citizenship. Just so, you have to be a citizen of heaven in order to qualify for the race that Paul speaks about.

However, there is this difference: *All* citizens of heaven are enrolled in this race. This is not optional; there are no other events offered during this time frame. You do not run this race to get to heaven; you run this race in order to receive the prize. This race began on the day you accepted Christ as your Savior.

Second, this is one race in which everyone has the potential of winning, for we are not competing with others, but with ourselves. We will be judged individually by God. To be determined is the question of what we did with what God gave us. Thus we all have our own personal finish line, our own personal coach, and our own personal final judgment.

## RULES OF THE RACE

Some people don't compete in sports because they fear failure. The humiliation of coming in last is just too much for those who are sensitive to public opinion. But fearful or not, this is one race we run every day. We are best served by shirking our fears and running as best we can. Yes, this is one race you and I can win.

What are those rules that make great athletes and thus make "great" Christians? Each of us can translate them into daily living.

## Discipline

When Paul speaks of those who compete in the games he uses the Greek word *agōnizomai,* from which we get our word *agonize.* "Everyone who *agonizes* in the games . . ." You and I are simply unable to grasp the hours of agony that go into athletic conditioning.

In August drive past a football field and watch the young athletes sweating under the hot sun. Clad in heavy clothes, padding, and a helmet, their faces grimace with distress and even pain. If they did this because their lives were threatened we might understand. What is difficult for some of us to grasp is that they do this voluntarily. All for a trophy that will be kept in a glass case and soon be forgotten in this life, and most assuredly not remembered in the next. They voluntarily want to play, and they will torture themselves in order to win.

Athletes must give up the bad and the good and strive for only the best. They must say no to parties and late nights. They cannot have the luxury of any personal enjoyment that conflicts with their ability to concentrate and to practice. Every distraction must be eschewed. I'm told that Mike Singletary of the Chicago Bears would work out with his team, then go home and do more exercises. Then, late at night when the house was quiet, he would watch videos of opposing teams to see how he might win against them.

Translate that into the disciplines of living the Christian life. Imagine the spurt of growth we would enjoy if we were to memorize Scripture, pray, and study the opposition with the same intensity as athletes attack their game. Just think of what would happen if we were to hone our spiritual sensitivities, our spiritual appetites, and our spiritual muscles. We could take on the world.

Samson is a good example of someone who didn't discipline his body. He apparently broke his Nazarite vow when he touched the dead carcass and ate the honey that was hidden in it. He played with temptation, and eventually it ensnared him. Far from bringing his body into subjection, he followed its desires wherever they led him.

We've all met people who are gifted and even love God, but they will accomplish only a fraction of what they might do for God. The reason is that they are satisfied with too little. They are in the race, but they don't want to pay the price of winning.

There are many ways to fail in the Christian life. But all of them begin with lack of discipline, a conscious decision to take the easy route. Paul says, "I discipline my body and bring it under control." The lie is that the body cannot be disciplined, for indeed it can, especially with the help of the Holy Spirit, who gives us self-control.

I'm not asking you to add to your busy and cluttered life, but rather to substitute the spiritual disciplines in favor of the priorities you have adopted. If you had to be on dialysis every day because of kidney malfunction, you would find the time to do it. We must approach our walk with God with the same single-minded determination. Paul says, "This one thing I do!" not "These forty things I dabble in."

If you struggle with discipline, begin with this:

- Spend twenty minutes in prayer and meditation every morning before 9:00.
- Read a chapter of a good Christian book each day.

- Join a group of believers (Bible study class, prayer group, etc.) for fellowship and accountability.
- Learn to share your faith, and take the opportunities that God brings along your path.

Discipline itself does not produce godliness. We are not made spiritual by being "under the law," depending on our own strength to win God's approval. Rather, the purpose of these disciplines is *that we might learn to draw our strength from Christ.*

## Direction

Two different sports help us understand what is needed to win an athletic contest: running and boxing. "Therefore I run in such a way, as not without aim; I box in such a way, as not beating the air" (1 Corinthians 9:26). Imagine an official firing the gun to start the 100-meter dash and the runners all heading in different directions! A sun lover runs toward the west, another fond of mountains runs toward the east, and a third heads toward the sea. Each would be expending maximum energy, but none would win the race. Only those headed toward the finish line would qualify for the prize.

Or, says Paul, consider a boxer. If he throws punches that never hit his opponent, he is wasting his energy. If the opponent takes no hits, it matters not how fast the swing or how powerful the punch. Paul would have none of this for himself; he ran toward the goal, and he boxed so as to make every blow count.

Elsewhere, he returned to the need to keep one's eyes on the goal, to keep one's eyes fastened on Christ.

Not that I have already obtained it, or have already become perfect, but I press on in order that I may lay hold of that for which also I was laid hold of by Christ Jesus. . . . I press on toward the goal for the prize of the upward call of God in Christ Jesus. (Philippians 3:12–14)

Paul says he *strains* toward the goal, *grasping* for what lies ahead. No wasted energy; no tangents and detours. He will win because he keeps the finish line clearly in mind. In fact, the goal is his consuming passion.

Growing up on a farm, I knew how important it was to plow a straight furrow, especially when beginning a new field. To do so, my father would chose an object in the distance and drive the tractor toward it, keeping his eyes on the "goal." There is a story, perhaps true, of a farmer who chose his target and drove carefully toward it, but when looking back discovered that the furrow curved behind him. The story goes that he had actually fastened his eyes on a cow in the distance, and as she walked around the pasture he had followed her movements!

The goal you choose will determine how straight a line your life leaves behind. Many a man has left a crooked furrow because he chose a temporal target. "I want to be a millionaire by the time I'm thirty!" The man who chose that goal lived to see it fulfilled, but he was also divorced by the age of twenty-six!

Moses left an enduring legacy because he chose an enduring goal.

By faith Moses, when he had grown up, refused to be called the son of Pharaoh's daughter; choosing rather to endure ill-treatment with the people of God, than to enjoy the passing pleasures of sin; considering the reproach of Christ greater riches than the treasures of Egypt; for he was looking to the reward. (Hebrews 11:24–26)

*Looking toward the reward!* He had a clear view that reached well beyond Egypt and the wilderness of Sinai. He saw the eternal reward and decided to go for it. Choosing this course was more difficult than herding sheep in the desert, but it was worth it. He did not confuse the invisible with the imaginary; he knew that heaven was more real than earth could ever be. He could see more than his contemporaries.

Our best example, however, is Christ Himself. "Fixing our eyes on Jesus, the author and perfecter of faith, who for the joy set before Him endured the cross, despising the shame, and has sat down at the right hand of the throne of God" (Hebrews 12:2). He too saw beyond this life into the next. He was motivated by the prize of sitting at the right hand of God the Father. Focus is everything. Every one of us should be able to state our goals, our most fervent ambitions. We must strive toward that which will endure.

While bobbing in a boat in Lake Michigan, I became nauseated until my friend encouraged me to choose a building on the shore and keep my eyes fixed on it. I chose the Sears Tower and discovered in a few moments that I felt better. He explained that the motion of a boat confuses our balance system if we look at the very object that is causing our movement. But we can handle the ups and downs if our eyes have a fixed object that is unmoved by our own vacillations.

We all have our days when we must say, "Today I will remember the goal; I will focus on Christ no matter what storm might come my way!"

### Determination

We've already referred to the passage in the book of Hebrews that tells us how to run the race. There we are given the rule book on how to run successfully. "Therefore, since we have so great a cloud of witnesses surrounding us, let us also lay aside every encumbrance, and the sin which so easily entangles us, and let us run with endurance the race that is set before us" (Hebrews 12:1).

You've heard Bible teachers say that this "cloud of witnesses" is a reference to those who have gone to heaven and are now watching us here on earth. But, in context, it is clear that the witnesses are the heroes of Hebrews 11, and *we are motivated, not because they see us, but because we see them!*

Specifically, we look back to men like Abraham, Joseph, and Moses and conclude that if they could run the race successfully, so can we. We learn from them that endurance is always possible if we remember where we are headed. We are to glance at these heroes and gaze on Jesus.

What are the rules of the race?

First, we must *keep our weight down*. We are to "lay aside every weight." Some people have to join a spiritual Weight Watchers group. There are some things that might not be sins, but weights, those habits and actions that take time and energy from that which is better.

Second, we are to *keep our feet free*. We must be free from the sin that does so easily "entangle" us. Sin tangles our feet, makes us stumble, and eventually will cause us to lose the race. Just think of the many people who began with a small weight or sin and ended up wounded on the sideline of the racetrack.

Those of us who are still in the race have an obligation to help those who have stumbled so that they too can cross the finish line.

In the 1992 Olympics, Derek Redmond of Great Britain popped his hamstring in the 400-meter semifinal heat. He limped and hobbled around half the Olympic Stadium track. The sight of his son's distress was too much for Jim Redmond, who had been sitting near the top row of the stadium packed with 65,000 people. He rushed down flights of stairs and blew past security people, who challenged his lack of credentials to be on the track.

"I wasn't interested in what they were saying," he said of the security guards. He caught up to his son on the top of the final curve, some 120 meters from the finish. He put one arm around Derek's waist, another around his left wrist. Then they did a three-legged hobble toward the finish line.

Derek had no chance of winning a medal, but his determination earned him the respect of the crowd. His father said, "He worked eight years for this. I wasn't going to let him not finish." Whether or not his father knew it, he was acting biblically.

"Therefore, strengthen the hands that are weak and the knees that are feeble, and make straight paths for your feet, so that the limb which is lame may not be put out of joint, but rather be healed" (Hebrews 12:12–13). Some people have to be helped across the finish line. Some have stumbled over their own feet; others have been tripped by family members and so-called friends. We must help those who have fallen into the snares of the devil; we must lift up the fallen, bind up their wounds, and help them on their journey toward home.

Determination will do it.

## MAKING IT TO THE FINISH LINE

Every runner knows the danger of distractions and potholes. We not only have to know how to win, but we must also know why many people have lost the race.

Please remember that chapter divisions in the Bible are not inspired! Paul does not conclude his thoughts about winning the race at the end of 1 Corinthians 9, but continues his thought into the next chapter: "For I do not want you to be unaware, brethren" (10:1). That little word *for* is a bridge that continues Paul's warning.

In chapter 9 Paul says, "I buffet my body and make it my slave, lest possibly, after I have preached to others, I myself should be disqualified" (v. 27). He feared that even he might lose the race!

When he begins chapter 10 he uses the Israelites in the desert as an illustration of those who lost the race. These were people redeemed out of Egypt; they had crossed the Red Sea and had experienced the daily provision of God, and yet they fell short of the prize.

First, Paul speaks of the blessings they enjoyed. They were given all they needed to run successfully.

> For I do not want you to be unaware, brethren, that our fathers were all under the cloud, and all passed through the sea; and all were baptized into Moses in the cloud and in the sea; and all ate the same spiritual food; and all drank the same spiritual drink, for they were drinking from a spiritual rock which followed them; and the rock was Christ. (vv. 1–4)

Next, Paul describes their failure in the face of innumerable blessings. "Nevertheless, with most of them God was not well-pleased" (v. 5). Then follows a list of their sins: idolatry, immorality, and ingratitude. Many of these people were saved in the Old Testament sense of that word: They will be in heaven. Nevertheless, they were displeasing to God and will not win the prize.

The contrast is between their many undeserved blessings and their failures. They began the race with all the resources for the journey, yet they stumbled badly, far from the finish line. Not only did they not make it into Canaan, they never even lived successfully in the desert, where God supplied all of their needs.

The same sins beset us today. Our only hope of winning is to repent; indeed, our lives should be lived with an attitude of repentance. Ask the Holy Spirit to show you the sins that might keep you from finishing well. If Paul feared that he might be disqualified, you and.I are most assuredly vulnerable.

"Say it ain't so, Ben."

That was how the venerable Canadian Broadcasting Corporation led its national radio news on Monday, September 27, 1988. Their national hero, Ben Johnson, had just tested positive for anabolic steroids and was stripped of the gold medal he had just won for breaking the record in the Olympic 100-meter race. Even as members of the Canadian Parliament were in the middle of flowery tributes to the "fastest man in the world," reports began to trickle in that Johnson had been disqualified. What made the embarrassment more acute was the fact that Johnson had just been extolled as a model "Say No to Drugs" athlete for Canadian youth.

Johnson learned that you can't win without obeying the rules. No matter how wonderfully we start, it is crossing the finish line well that counts.

We look back and say, "Abraham won; David won; Joseph won; so did a host of people who did not see deliverance but trusted God anyway." We can do the same! But let us always remember what it cost them.

Nothing fades as quickly as flowers. In the hot sunlight they last but a few hours. It was for such a wreath that the athletes competed in ancient Greece. Paul called it a "corruptible crown."

In contrast, there is an incorruptible crown given to those who serve Christ. It is guaranteed to last forever. We must covet the "prize of the high calling of God in Christ Jesus." Paul was not embarrassed to say that he desired to win the crown; he did not think it unspiritual to seek for the approval of Christ and the honor associated with it.

On a businessman's desk was this sign:

**In 20 years what will you wish you had done today?**
*Do it now!*

Do you want to win the race? Whatever it takes, just "Do it *now!*"

# $\mathscr{S}$TANDING IN LINE TO RECEIVE YOUR REWARD

Len was in the hospital, dying of cancer, when I had the privilege of explaining the gospel to him and he believed on Christ. During his remaining three weeks, he prayed, read his Bible, and was a blessing to those who visited him. He was not afraid to die but regretted that he had waited so long to become a born-again Christian.

What chance does he have to be rewarded by Christ since his works were so few and, for the most part, his life such a waste? Someone has said that a deathbed conversion is "burning a candle in the service of the devil and blowing the smoke in the eyes of God."

The thief on the cross had no opportunity to do good works. Perhaps he died giving praise to the One who had just promised him eternal life. That was something, but compared to a life of service, not much. Does God have a pay scale in heaven like we find in an employee handbook? Are we rewarded according to the number of days, hours, or years we serve? What happens to Christian young people killed in a car accident, or to infants who have not had the chance of doing even one good work?

Christ told a parable that has often been misinterpreted, but I believe it provides the clue to the questions we have just posed. The story comes to grips with the fairness and generosity of God and also the matter of our attitude in service. It ends with the surprise that "the last shall be first, and the first last" (Matthew 20:16).

Christ had just confronted a young rich man who was not willing to admit that he had a problem with being covetous; so Christ asked him to sell everything he had and give the money to the poor so that he would have treasure in heaven. But when the young man heard this statement, he went away grieved, "for he was one who owned much property" (Matthew 19:22).

Christ later explained to the disciples that it was very hard for a rich man to enter the kingdom; indeed, "it is easier for a camel to go through the eye of a needle, than for a rich man to enter the kingdom of God" (v. 24). Peter, bless him, thinking about what it cost the disciples to follow Christ, asked, "Behold, we have left everything and followed You; what then will there be for us?" (v. 27). Probably we would have had the same question on our minds but not the nerve to ask, "What's in it for me?"

We are the ones who are tempted to think that any consideration of rewards is self-centered. But Christ did not chide Peter for his question. After all, Christ Himself was motivated "for the joy set before Him" (Hebrews 12:2). Just as pleasing the Father entailed a reward, even so when we in turn please Christ we are promised a reward. It is not wrong for us to strive to be thought worthy of His approval.

Christ responds to Peter's question with a lofty promise.

> Truly I say to you, that you who have followed Me, in the regeneration when the Son of Man will sit on His glorious throne, you also shall sit upon twelve thrones, judging the twelve tribes of Israel. And everyone who has left houses or brothers or sisters or father or mother or children or farms for My name's sake, shall receive many times as much, and shall inherit eternal life. But many who are first will be last; and the last, first. (Matthew 19:28–30)

What a return on an investment! Mark quotes Christ as saying that such a person will receive "a hundred times as much now in the present age, houses and brothers and sisters and mothers and children and farms, along with persecutions; and in the age to come, eternal life" (10:30). Obviously, we cannot take this literally, since no one would want a hundred brothers, sisters, and mothers! Christ's point is simply that the rewards both in this life and the life to come will be out of proportion to the cost of discipleship. How would you like to put your money in a bank with a guaranteed interest of 10,000 percent!

Samuel Zwemer, famous missionary to the Muslims, lost two daughters, ages four and seven, within eight days of each other. The temperature soared regularly to 107 degrees in the coolest part of the verandah. His work was largely fruitless and fraught with great setbacks for him and his wife. Yet fifty years later, looking back on this period, he wrote, "The sheer joy of it all comes back. Gladly would I do it all over again."[1]

Many missionaries who have left houses, lands, and families bear witness to the fact that the joy of serving Christ makes up for the sacrifice. Piper writes: "If you give up a mother's nearby affection and concern, you get back one hundred times the affection and concern from the ever-present Christ. . . . If you give up the sense of at-homeness you had in your house, you get back one hundred times the comfort and security of knowing that your Lord owns every house and land and stream and tree on earth."[2]

We are asked to deny ourselves of the lesser good for the greater good. Paul was willing to say that everything was garbage in comparison to knowing Christ. And for such a commitment there is also an eternal reward. Someone has said that *the remuneration will be much greater than the renunciation.*

## CHRIST'S STORY

In Israel the grape harvest ripens near the end of September, and after that the rains begin to fall. There is only a short window of time, perhaps two weeks, when the grapes can be harvested. Understandably, vineyard owners often find extra help to harvest their produce quickly. An owner can go to the marketplace and find workers willing to be paid at the end of each day. Each hopes he will be hired.

"For the kingdom of heaven is like a landowner who went out early in the morning to hire laborers for his vineyard. And when he had agreed with the laborers for a denarius for the day, he sent them into his vineyard" (Matthew 20:1–2).

The owner went out at 6:00 A.M. and found a group of hired hands. After some negotiations, he hired them for the standard rate: a denarius per worker per day. Off they went into the fields, doing enough work to satisfy the demands of the contract.

But there was more work to be done. So the owner went out at nine o'clock, at noon, and even at five o'clock to hire others so that the harvest would be in by sundown. He hired as many as he needed to finish the job by the end of the day, at 6:00 P.M.

When the task was finished, he asked his foreman to line up the laborers to be paid. To the astonishment of everyone, the owner requested that those who came last would be paid first. "And when those hired about the eleventh hour [five in the afternoon] came, each one received a denarius" (v. 9).

Imagine! They worked one hour and received pay for the whole day! As they left they flashed the denarius they had been paid and word spread down the line about the generosity of the vineyard owner. The last-hired workers thrilled at the prospect of having a good supper with some money to spare. This was a man for whom they would gladly work again!

Of course, the early birds who were standing in line could hardly wait to get their wages. They did a mental calculation: If the pay is one denarius per hour, then they should receive twelve denarii. And if not twelve, they would be satisfied with ten.

They were unprepared for the disappointment that awaited them. Word spread that those who came at three o'clock in the afternoon also received a denarius; similarly, those who had arrived at noon and even at nine o'clock received but a single denarius! And now the early birds were next in line. "And when those hired first came, they thought that they would receive more; and they also received each one a denarius" (v. 10).

Unfair!

"And when they received it, they grumbled at the landowner, saying, 'These last men have worked only one hour, and you have made them equal to us who have borne the burden and the scorching heat of the day'" (vv. 11–12). If they had known this was going to happen, they also would have come at 5:00 P.M. Why not do as little as you must to get what others are getting? If they were living in our day, they would have complained to the labor relations board.

But the owner had a ready reply. "'Friend, I am doing you no wrong; did you not agree with me for a denarius? Take what is yours and go your way, but I wish to give to this last man the same as to you. Is it not lawful for me to do what I wish with what is my own? Or is your eye envious because I am generous?' Thus the last shall be first, and the first last" (vv. 13–16).

So much for that.

## THE INTERPRETATION

How shall we interpret this story?

Some have thought that the denarius represents salvation. Thus, whether one is saved early in life or later, one still receives the same gift. The man who believes on Christ on his deathbed receives the same eternal life as the person who has served God for many years.

But there are serious problems with this understanding of the story. Thankfully, we do not have to work to enter the vineyard, because none of us would be qualified. This is a parable about payment for work, not about salvation by grace.

Others have suggested that this parable teaches that it is not the length of time you work, but how *hard* you work. Those who came early took long breaks, chatted while they picked the grapes, and took a three-hour lunch. So those who came at 5:00 did just as much as those who entered the vineyard at sunrise.

But we have no evidence that those who came later were better workers, while the early ones loafed. Indeed, when the early birds complained, "We have borne the burden and the scorching heat of the day," the owner did not dispute their claim.

A third interpretation says that everyone will receive the same reward. Whether you enter the vineyard as a faithful worker or a self-centered opportunist, you will in the end be rewarded the same. So the judgment seat of Christ involves nothing more than having us line up and receive our denarius.

But this cannot be Christ's meaning. Indeed, the very context of the story proves otherwise! Christ has just assured Peter and the other disciples that they would be generously rewarded because they had left all to follow Him. They would rule over the twelve tribes of Israel in the kingdom.

And, if we should envy these disciples, we are also promised that we can receive a reward if we are willing to leave father and mother and carry our cross. Whatever the reward might be, Christ said it would be much greater than whatever we give up. Clearly, everyone does not receive the same reward. Why would so many passages in the New Testament speak of rewards if we all will be equally honored when we stand before Christ?

Perhaps there is a better interpretation.

Remember that the Jews received the first invitation to the kingdom. Back in Genesis God promised Abraham that he would be great and through him all the nations of the earth would be blessed. This began a series of covenants and promises that would culminate in the coming of Christ and the eventual establishment of the kingdom. Now the Jews resented the Gentiles, who were invited by Christ into the vineyard. These newcomers were happy for the privilege and were being blessed by God.

When Jesus was criticized for befriending sinners, he told the familiar story of the prodigal son who went into the far country and squandered his living. When he returned home, the elder brother resented the generosity of the father toward his wayward sibling. After all, he was the hard worker who kept the farm going. And now the father was rewarding this scoundrel for just coming home!

The elder brother had taken his father for granted. He worked on the farm, not because he loved the father, but because of what he could get out of him. He thought that rewards should be doled out according to a payroll time chart. So much money for so many hours. And now his wayward brother comes home and the father showers him with irrational attention and joy. That was too much for the boy who had stayed home and did all the hard work on the farm.

That, I believe, is the attitude of those who came to the vineyard at 6:00 A.M. We read, "And when he had *agreed* with the laborers for a denarius for the day, he sent them into his vineyard" (v. 2, italics added). They negotiated for all they could get. The others who came later served without an agreement. The vineyard owner assured them, "You too go into the vineyard, and whatever is right I will give you," and they trusted him (v. 4). It is not just a matter of how long you serve but the *attitude* with which you serve that counts. What is more, for those who serve well, the owner pays beyond their wildest dreams.

## THE LESSONS TO BE LEARNED

There are several lessons that emerge from the parable, and in uncovering them we are led to the heart of what Christ attempted to communicate.

### We Should Serve in Faith, Without a Contract

Haddon Robinson says that one day his son came in from the hot Texas sun and exclaimed, "Dad, I've mowed the lawn!" which, of course, is another way of saying, "Pay me!"

His father asked, "How much do you think your work is worth?" The boy refused to answer.

When pressed, he continued to evade the question, and his father insisted, "Why don't you name your price?"

To which the boy replied, "I know that if you make the decision you will give me more than I would ever ask!"

Those who came early to the vineyard named their price; the others did not. We can imagine the tone of the negotiations at sunrise. They wanted to know exactly what was in it for them. They would not set foot in the vineyard without knowing in advance what they would get in return.

The others were satisfied with the words of the vineyard owner, "Whatever is right I will give you." They felt honored to be asked to serve, and whatever the owner paid them they believed would be sufficient. They gave him the freedom to make the choice.

I've heard Christians say, "I promised God that if He gave me a better job, I would begin to tithe . . ." Or, "If God doesn't call me to Africa, I will get a good job and support ten missionaries . . ." Such bargains tie God's hands, and He cannot be generous with us. We must not try to make a deal with the Almighty; we should simply serve Him to the best of our ability and let Him worry about the results. We must seek His will and trust Him to do right by us.

We must never think we can make God obligated to us. Let us remember that God owes us nothing but eternal punishment. God has chosen to reward us, not because He owes us anything, but because He is generous. To *insist* that we receive some compensation is to miss the whole point of our Father-son relationship.

When we make a bargain with God, stipulating that He do business on our terms, we lose. He will be more gracious when we realize that He alone has the right to make the choice about our rewards. He invites us to rejoice in His promise that we will be rewarded, but He must determine what that reward will be. With His decision we shall be satisfied.

## We Should Serve in Submission, Not Envy

Those early birds eyed the latecomers, envying the generous pay they had received. They resented the fact that the owner had given these loafers more money than they deserved. The vineyard owner responded, "Is it not lawful for me to do what I wish with what is my own? Or is your eye envious because I am generous?" (v. 15). Unfortunately, we all too easily fall into the sin of comparison, resenting those who are above us and despising those who are beneath us. Read the pages of church history and you will soon discover that many of the conflicts were not doctrinal, but personal. Sometimes God's blessings were so unevenly distributed that one Christian envied another, scheming for his brother's demise. How much better if we could rejoice in the exaltation of others!

A friend of mine asked me if I ever had noticed how often God puts His hand on the wrong person! His point, of course, is that God often blesses some people more abundantly than we would if we were the Almighty! To be envious, or to complain that our part in the vineyard is not as great as that of someone else, is to miss the heart of service to Christ.

Charles Ryrie, author of the study notes in the *Ryrie Study Bible,* says that one day he was on a plane when the flight attendants asked some of the coach-class passengers to move into the first-class section. Unfortunately, he was not chosen to be among the fortunate. He resented having to stay put while others were asked to move toward the spacious seats.

While he sat quietly, bristling about his plight, he recalled this parable and read it. He paraphrased the words: "Friend, I am doing you no wrong. Did you not agree with American Airlines for a coach seat? Do you not have a coach seat? Is it not lawful for American Airlines to do as it wills with those who are its own? If it wishes to give first-class treatment to second-class passengers, is your eye envious because American Airlines is generous?"

We must not become envious if God is more generous to some people than we think He should be! Indeed, if He were not generous, none of us would be saved and not a one of us would be rewarded. Let us be satisfied with our place in the vineyard, no matter how obscure or unappreciated. Since whatever we receive is undeserved, we should be grateful for any pay the owner grants us.

God is sovereign in who He chooses to save; He is sovereign in the distribution of privileges and gifts. And He is also sovereign in the rewards He chooses to give us. Obviously, He does not act arbitrarily.

There is a connection between our service on earth and the rewards we shall receive in heaven. But we will receive so much more than we could ever hope for.

Indeed, this leads us to the heart of the parable.

## Our Reward Is Grace, Not Wages

In heaven there will be reversals: "Thus the last shall be first, and the first last" (v. 16). With these words Christ encapsulated the central teaching of the parable. Some who have come to the kingdom late might just be ahead of those who entered early in the day.

As we have already learned, the first reason for this reversal in rank is that God takes into account the attitude with which we serve. The person who comes to faith in Christ late in life and thus enters the vineyard late in the day does not have the same opportunity to do as many good deeds as the person who grew up in the faith. But if such a latecomer serves well, he will receive much more than he could ever expect. Perhaps a lifetime of pay for a month of service. Rewards are not based on the amount of *time* in the vineyard.

If the length of time one worked in the vineyard determined our reward, none of us would want to be a martyr! We would want to go on serving Christ to accumulate more good deeds. But the fact is that God determines how long we are in the vineyard. No one is penalized because his life is cut short.

The teenager killed in an accident, the man who receives Christ as Savior while on his deathbed—these shall receive more than they could possibly hope for. Perhaps even the infant will be graciously rewarded, based on what he or she might have done if given the opportunity. These shall be rewarded above those who served God out of a sense of duty, out of a legalistic heart without a loving touch. Thus the first shall be last and the last first.

Second, it is clear that the bottom line is that the reward we receive will not be equal pay for equal service. Rather, our reward will be a hundred times greater than any work we actually have done. God will pay the legalist who has worked for a fixed price, but in the end He will compensate far beyond expectations those who have trusted Him. Our relationship with Him is not just between master and slave, but between a Father who delights in sharing His inheritance and His obedient child.

In the end we shall receive much more than we have merited; in fact, as we have already learned, we "deserve" nothing. God will give us rewards that are totally out of proportion to the work we have done. Since no one "earns" rewards anyway, we shall receive the benefits of a gracious wage. We will have hearts of gratitude for all of eternity.

Henry C. Morrison and his wife, after serving for forty years in Africa, came home by boat. Theodore Roosevelt and his entourage were also aboard; there was much pomp and revelry. The president's arrival in New York was greeted with a great delegation and fanfare. But the Morrisons felt dejected, for there was no one there to meet them. As they thought about it, they realized that those who caroused on the ship, drinking and dancing, those who were famous—they had a rousing welcome. The missionaries did not.

Understandably, the couple felt resentment. But one day the joy of the Lord returned to Mr. Morrison. He explained to his wife that he had been praying, rehearsing one more time his indignation toward God.

"We are servants of the most High God and when we returned home there was no one to greet us; when those who are serving this world returned home they had a rousing welcome . . .

"Then," he said, "it was as if the Lord said to me, 'Just wait, *you aren't home yet!*'"

Whatever deprivations we have had here on earth, whatever loneliness we endure, whatever suffering comes our way for the sake of Christ—for this we shall be generously rewarded. We will stand amazed when we see that God gave us so much for so little!

We've been called to the vineyard at different times, but thanks be, we can count on being "paid" at the end of the day. And because of the generosity of the owner, some of the last shall be first and the first last. Of course, our reward will not be monetary. Rather, we shall have the joy of reigning with Christ. And it is to this ultimate reward we now turn.

## NOTES

1. John Piper, *Desiring God* (Portland, Ore.: Multnomah, 1986), 203.
2. Ibid., 199.

CHAPTER NINE

# REIGNING WITH
# CHRIST FOREVER

And they shall reign forever and ever."
So says the apostle John of the Lord's bond-servants
who serve Him in the New Jerusalem (Revelation
22:5). Ruling with Christ is God's ultimate intention
for believers; it is our highest possible privilege. "He
who overcomes, I will grant to him to sit down with
Me on My throne, as I also overcame and sat down
with My Father on His throne" (3:21).

Those who rule with Christ are overcomers, those
who have successfully conquered the challenges of
this life. They have weathered the storms and have
believed in God's promises against incredible odds.
They have willingly suffered for His name. They have
resisted the threefold seduction of pleasure, possessions, and power. These are the ones who genuinely
came to believe that "the world is passing away, and
also its lusts; but the one who does the will of God
abides forever" (1 John 2:17).

This is the company of believers who proved that they are *worthy* of the Savior. Three times Christ used that word in Matthew 10:37–38. Although we have quoted this passage previously, we are now prepared to look it in new light. "He who loves father or mother more than Me is not *worthy* of Me; and he who loves son or daughter more than Me is not *worthy* of Me. And he who does not take his cross and follow after Me is not *worthy* of Me" (italics added).

Paul exhorts us to "walk in a manner *worthy* of the calling with which you have been called" (Ephesians 4:1, italics added). And again, "So that you may walk in a manner *worthy* of the God who calls you into His own kingdom and glory" (1 Thessalonians 2:12, italics added). We are to prove ourselves worthy of our high calling. We are, says Iosif Ton, "formed, shaped and tested for reliability, and based on our degree of trustworthiness we are given a position of responsibility in the kingdom."[1]

We cannot emphasize too often that this is not a privilege which is "earned" in the usual sense of the word. It is a gift of immeasurable grace based on our temporal efforts on earth. As we have seen, rewards are determined by our response to the opportunities (whether great or small) that are presented to us.

## THE FATHER AND HIS SONS

Let us remind ourselves that God wants to produce character in us that is similar to that of Christ. The qualities seen in Him are the ones that make for greatness in the kingdom. As man, Christ was exalted because He had that in which the Father found His delight. These qualities are universally ignored by the world.

Many people in the health and wealth gospel

preach that we should live like a "king's kid." What they mean is that we should strive for money and enjoy it; after all, the children of a king are usually spoiled with all the amenities this world can provide.

What they forget is that Christ was the "King's kid" who lived a life that is directly opposite to what the health and wealth gospel promotes. He was born into poverty and lived without any investments in this world. And although God might not require the same form of self-denial for us, the fact is that Christ was as countercultural as one could possibly be. He modeled poverty and humility; and this, He taught, was the path to greatness.

Christ chided His disciples for confusing the blessings of the coming kingdom with the lifestyles of earth. If they wanted to be great tomorrow, fine; let them learn that this could only be achieved by taking the lowest roles today. Bonhoeffer was right when he said, "The figure of the Crucified invalidates all thought that takes success for its standard."

Christ had already promised the disciples that they would rule with Him in the coming kingdom, but this was not quite good enough for the mother of James and John. She came to Christ with her two sons in tow, requesting that they get to sit on Christ's left and right when the kingdom age got under way (Matthew 20:20–28). The conversation developed like this:

"Teacher, we want You to do for us whatever we ask of You."

"What do you want Me to do for you?"

"Grant that we may sit in Your glory, one on Your right, and one on Your left."

When the other ten disciples heard about this secret discussion they were indignant, angry that this request was made behind their backs. The other disciples wanted to compete for the two chairs next to Christ and His throne. Our Lord was not upset with their request, but He did point out that they did not understand the nature of true greatness in the kingdom.

First, He asked them whether they were willing to suffer with Him, earning their place in the kingdom. "You do not know what you are asking for. Are you able to drink the cup that I am about to drink?" (v. 22). They replied that they were able. This is the first test of greatness, the ability to suffer with Christ. Indeed, He was perfected through suffering, and we should be too. Greatness is not ease or luxury; it is pain and tears. As Alexander Maclaren said, every step on the pathway to spiritual progress will be marked by the bloody footprints of wounded self-love.

Christ apparently agreed that they had the determination to suffer with Him. He continues, "My cup you shall drink; but to sit on My right and on My left, this is not Mine to give, but it is for those for whom it has been prepared by My Father" (v. 23). The Holy Spirit within us gives us a willingness to suffer, despite our natural hesitations and fears.

We do all we can to prevent suffering, but God nevertheless brings trials into our lives. Although He heals some from disease, many experience years of relentless pain and agony. Every affliction, it is said, comes with a message from the heart of God. Looked at from the standpoint of eternity, it is a gift to be cherished, for it enhances our eternal joy and honor.

But there is a second quality needed en route to the throne. Christ points out that greatness in the kingdom means humility and servanthood.

> You know that the rulers of the Gentiles lord it over them, and their great men exercise authority over

them. It is not so among you, but whoever wishes to
become great among you shall be your servant, and
whoever wishes to be first among you shall be your
slave; just as the Son of Man did not come to be
served, but to serve, and to give His life a ransom for
many. (vv. 25–28)

The law of the kingdom is directly opposite to that
of the world. In the world, greatness is determined by
the number of people whom you rule; to rule over ten
thousand is better than to rule over a thousand. In the
kingdom, greatness is determined by the number of
people you serve. Humility is the badge of highest
honor. Indeed, Christ Himself was exalted because He
came not to be served, but to serve and to "give His
life a ransom for many" (v. 28).

Paul makes an explicit connection between Christ's
humility and future exaltation. "And being found in
appearance as a man, He humbled Himself by becoming obedient to the point of death, even death on a
cross. Therefore also God highly exalted Him, and
bestowed on Him the name which is above every
name" (Philippians 2:8–9). His lowly submission to
God is the reason why God highly exalted Him. He
taught us that *the way up is down.*

Incredibly, Christ's servant role will continue in the
kingdom! Indeed, it appears as if He shall serve us
when we sit down to dinner! Christ exhorts the disciples to be ready for His return, to be the first to open
the door to Him when He knocks. "Blessed are those
slaves whom the master shall find on the alert when
he comes; truly I say to you, that he will gird himself
to serve, and have them recline at the table, and will
come up and wait on them" (Luke 12:37). Serving is
not just fit for earth, but also for heaven. The humility

of Christ toward us should bring tears to our eyes. As Augustine said, "God humbled Himself, while man remains proud."

We serve as a stepping-stone to greatness, but serving itself is greatness; it is being like Christ. Ironically, if you want to rule with Christ, don't try to seek this reward by finding a lofty position and using it as a stepping-stone to something greater. Find a towel, a basin, and some dirty feet and take the role of a servant. Within God's good time, He may see fit to give you greater responsibility. "Humble yourselves, therefore, under the mighty hand of God, that He may exalt you at the proper time" (1 Peter 5:6). To want exaltation is fair enough, but it can only be achieved through humility. Paradoxically, *the very thing we seek, greatness, is found through its opposite, humility!*

If we wish to be great in the kingdom, we must begin by serving our spouses, our children, and any needy person we can help. We must die to our natural desire to be served and begin to serve, taking the initiative in meeting the needs of others. And if poor health or such limitations prevent us from active service, let us serve others through our prayers and encouragement.

Michelangelo, it is said, looked at a block of marble and said, "I see an angel in that block of marble." God goes into the quarry of sin, takes rough stones, and hews them into the shape of Christ. He is pleased when He looks at us and we remind Him of His only begotten Son, who was a servant.

## THE NATURE OF REWARDS

When we specifically ask what rewards are, the Bible gives a variety of descriptions. The book of Revelation is filled with figures of speech that help us peer though the window to see what the inheritance of the faithful might be.

## Special Privileges

Just contemplate the generosity of God:

- "To him who overcomes, I will grant to eat of the tree of life, which is in the paradise of God" (Revelation 2:7).
- "He who overcomes shall not be hurt by the second death" (Revelation 2:11).
- "To him who overcomes, to him I will give some of the hidden manna, and I will give him a white stone, and a new name written on the stone which no one knows but he who receives it" (Revelation 2:17).
- "And he who overcomes, and he who keeps My deeds until the end, to him I will give authority over the nations" (Revelation 2:26).
- "He who overcomes, I will make him a pillar in the temple of My God, and he will not go out from it anymore; and I will write upon him the name of My God, and the name of the city of My God, the new Jerusalem, which comes down out of heaven from My God, and My new name" (Revelation 3:12).

We need not pause to interpret such passages except to say that all of them speak of special privileges or intimate fellowship with Christ. Whether it is eating, receiving a secret name, or becoming a pillar in the temple of God, all of these speak of close proximity to our Lord in heaven. John Bunyan was right when he said, "He who is most in the bosom of God, and who so acts for Him here, he is the man who will be best able to enjoy most of God in the kingdom of heaven."[2]

Some Bible scholars insist that all Christians are overcomers because these passages in Revelation do not speak of what happens to the "nonovercomers." However, the warnings to these churches make clear that some of the believers were not overcoming in their witness for Christ. Indeed, the promises are never made to the church in general, but to specific individuals within the congregation. Thus the singular pronoun: "*he* who overcomes."

We are not well served by a theology that does not recognize the possibility of serious moral and doctrinal defection on the part of believers. We've learned that Paul himself beat his body lest he be "disqualified." He lived with the healthy fear that he could end in disgrace and failure. Think about the man in the church of Corinth about whom Paul wrote, "I have decided to deliver such a one to Satan for the destruction of his flesh, that his spirit may be saved in the day of the Lord Jesus" (1 Corinthians 5:5). The same could be said for Paul's companions Hymenaeus and Alexander, whom he also "delivered over to Satan, so that they may be taught not to blaspheme" (1 Timothy 1:20).

Of course, these believers were legally perfect in Christ; they were overcomers, judicially speaking, for they were accepted by God on the merit of Christ. But they were not overcomers in their practical experience. God exhorts us to be overcomers of the world and its multifaceted temptations because He delights in seeing us be victorious in daily living. The fact that we are secure in Christ does not mean that we are incapable of serious failure, and with it the loss of rewards.

If you are not convinced that there will be important distinctions in the kingdom, remember that Christ spoke about those who would be "great" in the kingdom and others who would be "least" in the kingdom. Again I emphasize that there will not be two camps in heaven, the haves and the have-nots. Rather, there are probably many different levels of responsibility because there are so many different levels of obedience and disobedience.

Rewards, particularly ruling with Christ, should not be taken as a foregone conclusion for all believers. We have observed that almost every time reigning with Christ is mentioned, it is always conditional. Successful suffering, overcoming, and faithfulness are generally spoken of as the qualifications. With these come special honors.

## Special Honors

Rewards are not only privileges, but also honors. Since the Scriptures speak of certain crowns being given to the faithful, some people believe that our eternal rewards are actual crowns that we will gladly lay at Christ's feet. This has given rise to the idea that our rewards or lack of them are really quite unimportant eternally. Whether we have one or many, we cast them at the feet of Christ at a great ceremony and then everyone gets on with eternity, enjoying essentially the same privileges.

> The twenty-four elders will fall down before Him who sits on the throne, and will worship Him who lives forever and ever, and will cast their crowns before the

151

throne, saying, "Worthy art Thou, our Lord and our God, to receive glory and honor and power; for Thou didst create all things, and because of Thy will they existed, and were created." (Revelation 4:10–11)

If we are given actual crowns in heaven, I'm sure that we shall gladly lay them at Christ's feet. But it is wrong to think that our rewards are crowns and nothing more. If we join the elders in casting our crowns before Him, I believe He shall give them back to us so we can join Him in ruling "forever and ever" (Revelation 22:5). Whatever might happen to the crowns, our rewards are eternal. Rewards are primarily not medallions, but specific honors.

Christ spoke of rewards as being "repayment," or of having "treasures," or of ruling with Him (as in the case of the disciples). Paul and John use the terminology of "crowns," but I believe that they intend this to be symbolic of our privilege of ruling with Christ. They would, I believe, be quite surprised that some interpreters think that our rewards will officially end when we throw our crowns at Christ's feet.

Although all crowns are based on faithfulness, there are different ways to be faithful. Enduring persecution might gain one person kingdom rule, whereas suffering with leukemia successfully might gain another the same privilege. Or perhaps single-minded generosity will introduce us to "the true riches."

Also, it is possible to win more than one crown. This is another indication that we should not make crowns equal to rewards. It would be odd indeed to try to fit five crowns on the same head! As you read through this list, you will see that although it might not be possible for one person to win them all, one could certainly have more than one.

What are some of the crowns? In the New Testament there are two words for "crown." *Stephanos* is a wreath crown, and *diadem* is a royal crown, the kind that Christ wears. In the passages listed below, the word *stephanos* is used, a crown given to winners.

### 1. *The Crown of Rejoicing*

The people we have led to Christ and nurtured in the faith are a "crown." Paul wrote, "For who is our hope or joy or crown of exultation? Is it not even you, in the presence of our Lord Jesus at His coming? For you are our glory and joy" (1 Thessalonians 2:19–20). This is another clue that crowns are to be understood as honors rather than a literal crown made of some cosmic metal. Meeting people we have known on earth will be a crown.

### 2. *The Crown of Glory*

For elders who serve well, there is special recognition. Peter wrote:

> Therefore, I exhort the elders among you, as your fellow elder and witness of the sufferings of Christ, and a partaker also of the glory that is to be revealed, shepherd the flock of God among you, exercising oversight not under compulsion, but voluntarily, according to the will of God; and not for sordid gain, but with eagerness; nor yet as lording it over those allotted to your charge, but proving to be examples to the flock. And when the Chief Shepherd appears, you will receive the unfading crown of glory. (1 Peter 5:1–4)

Again, this is an expression of reward for faithfulness. We should not think that elders will be identified in heaven because they are wearing a crown that is distinguishable from others. Faithfulness in being a good shepherd on earth will merit special honors from the Good Shepherd in heaven.

3. *The Crown of Righteousness*

We've already learned that this crown is given to those who eagerly await Christ's appearing.

> For I am already being poured out as a drink offering, and the time of my departure has come. I have fought the good fight, I have finished the course, I have kept the faith; in the future there is laid up for me the crown of righteousness, which the Lord, the righteous Judge, will award to me on that day; and not only to me, but also to all who have loved His appearing. (2 Timothy 4:6–8)

All Christians receive the righteousness of Christ; without it, heaven would be lost. This crown is a reference to a special enjoyment of righteousness because of a love for Christ. Paul wants us to understand that a love for Christ will attract the attention of Him whom we love.

4. *The Crown of Life*

This crown is given to those who successfully endure the sufferings associated with temptation. "Blessed is a man who perseveres under trial; for once he has been approved, he will receive the crown of life, which the Lord has promised to those who love Him" (James 1:12).

The same crown is given to martyrs. "Do not fear what you are about to suffer. Behold, the devil is about to cast some of you into prison, that you may be tested, and you will have tribulation ten days. Be faithful until death, and I will give you the crown of life" (Revelation 2:10). Blessed are those who will not give up their allegiance to Christ despite the seductions within the soul or the trials found in our path. The trials of the bride are carefully thought out by the Bridegroom! Remember, the goal is faithfulness that we might be found worthy to reign.

All Christians are given eternal life. The crown of life obviously refers to a certain enjoyment of life because of faithfulness in enduring the hardships of life. Thus we see again that the crowns are symbolic of privileges and accompanying responsibilities.

5. *Crown of Mastery*

This is a crown given to those who run the race successfully, "They then do it," says Paul, "to receive a perishable wreath, but we an imperishable" (1 Corinthians 9:25b). This is given to those who have paid the price of sacrifice and discipline in running the Christian race. This is a crown fit for those who have mastered the sins of the body, having brought it into subjection.

## Special Responsibilities

Now we come to the final drama, the end to which the plan of salvation was directed. As we stated in an earlier chapter, God's eternal purpose was to find a bride who would rule with Christ, joining Him on the throne of the universe.

Over what shall we rule? What will our responsibilities be? Of course we cannot answer these questions in detail, but the Scriptures give us sufficient teaching to enable us to glimpse into the future. We see through a glass darkly, but thankfully, we *do* see.

Our first opportunity for rule will be over the earth in the millennial kingdom. Christ promised twelve thrones to the twelve apostles, but there may also be other thrones that will be occupied. If not, we will be given various responsibilities, assignments commensurate with our faithfulness while living on this planet. Daniel the prophet foresaw the legacy of the saints in kingdom rule: "But the saints of the Highest One will receive the kingdom and possess the kingdom forever, for all ages to come" (Daniel 7:18).

After the millennial kingdom, a new phase of eternity begins. The New Jerusalem will come down from God out of heaven. Our responsibilities of reigning with Christ will continue, but in a new sphere. "And there shall no longer be any night; and they shall not have need of the light of a lamp nor the light of the sun, because the Lord God shall illumine them; and they shall reign forever and ever" (Revelation 22:5).

This rule extends for all eternity. Paul argued that one of the reasons Christians should not take one another to court is because this world is practice for greater responsibility in the world to come. He writes, "Or do you not know that the saints will judge the world? And if the world is judged by you, are you not competent to constitute the smallest law courts? Do you not know that we shall judge angels? How much more, matters of this life?" (1 Corinthians 6:2–3).

We shall judge angels, not in the sense that they need to be brought to justice, but rather in the sense that we shall rule over them. This most probably is what makes Satan so furious. The fact that sinful human beings, who sided with him in Eden, will be exalted above the angelic realm of which he was at one time a member is more than he can bear.

## RULING FOREVER

When scientists began to understand the size of the universe, man's place in the cosmos seemed to diminish. After all, if the universe is 20 billion light years in diameter, and if there are stars millions of times greater than our earth, man is but a speck of dust on the cosmic landscape. We ask with David, "What is man, that Thou dost take thought of him? And the son of man, that Thou dost care for him?" (Psalm 8:4).

The discovery of the immensity of the universe does not diminish but actually magnifies man's role in the cosmos. For if Christ is to rule over all things and we are to reign with Him, then we will be ruling over all the galaxies, affirming Christ's Lordship over the whole universe.[3]

Scientists tell us that there are as many stars in the universe as there are grains of sand on the beaches of the world. It is unthinkable that so much as one of them would wander aimlessly in space without contributing to the greater glory of God. In a way that we cannot comprehend, all things will be in subjection to Christ, and we shall be a part of His eternal rule.

Daniel predicted the final destiny of those who belong to the Almighty. "And those who have insight will shine brightly like the brightness of the expanse of heaven, and those who lead the many to righteousness, like the stars forever and ever" (Daniel 12:3). Unworthy though we are, there we will be, reigning in accordance with Christ's instructions. Perhaps all believers will shine like stars, but some will shine more brightly than others.

We can imagine a factory worker, ignored here on earth, now exalted to the dizzy heights of rule with Christ on a celestial throne. And here is a woman, an invalid, who endured the physical pain of Parkinson's disease and the emotional pain of childhood trauma as a gift from God to refine her faith. She prayed for others, gave encouragement, and lived her life with implicit faith in her Lord. Now, in her resplendent body, she rules, not taking advantage of her new authority, but in submission to Christ. At last she understands what Paul meant when he said, "For I consider that the sufferings of this present time are not worthy to be compared with the glory that is to be revealed to us" (Romans 8:18). The person she was on earth determined the rewards she now enjoys.

In 1881 King Charles of Romania did not have a crown; he requested that one be made from the metal captured by the nation in battle. It was bought and paid for by Romanian lives. Just so, the crown we wear will be the result of our successful suffering with Christ on earth. He suffered immeasurably in our behalf that we might be in heaven forever. Our suffering adds nothing to the completed work He did on our behalf. But the lives we live after He has saved us prepare whatever crown(s) we will enjoy in heaven.

What if there are some Christians who do not get to rule with Christ, or are given lesser authority in the heavenly kingdom? They will not envy those above them. In fact, Jonathan Edwards says, in heaven we shall be so free of sin that we will rejoice in the exaltation of others as though it were our own! We will not regret that others are above us, but we will regret that we did not serve the Savior to the best of our ability.

Somewhere I read a story about a wealthy couple who had a son they dearly loved. Unfortunately, the mother died, leaving the care of the boy with the father. He knew that he needed help to raise the lad, so he enlisted the aid of a housekeeper, who came to take care of the boy. She came to love him as if he were her own son.

The boy was stricken with a disease and died at a young age. Soon after, perhaps because of a broken heart, the father also died. And, because no will was found, the decision was made to auction his personal effects to the highest bidder.

The housekeeper attended the auction, not because she could afford the expensive furniture or the pricey antiques. She came because she wanted a picture of the boy that hung in the living room. When the auctioneer got to it, it sold for but a few cents.

When the woman took the picture home, she noticed a piece of paper attached to the back. It was the father's last will and testament, written in his own handwriting, which read simply, "I will all of my inheritance to anyone who loved my son enough to buy this picture."

God the Father loves His Son. And if we love Him, the Father will stop at nothing to bless us, even granting us the privilege of ruling with Him. "He who did not spare His own Son, but delivered Him up for us all, how will He not also with Him freely give us all things?" (Romans 8:32).

Yes, when we receive Christ we are graciously rewarded. And for those who are faithful there is the prospect of ruling with Him forever. That God should be so gracious to those who once were His enemies is the essence of the gospel. It is here that we encounter the mystery of God's matchless grace.

Come with me to the city of Rome with its opulent cathedrals, sculptures, and monuments. Survey the pyramids of Egypt and the splendor of the Palace of Versailles. Visit the skyscrapers of New York and the exclusive shops along Chicago's Michigan Avenue. Spend your life studying works of art and the great literature of the world.

Now compare these possessions with our eternal inheritance. The contrast is stark and gripping.

159

But the day of the Lord will come like a thief, in which the heavens will pass away with a roar and the elements will be destroyed with intense heat, and the earth and its works will be burned up. Since all these things are to be destroyed in this way, what sort of people ought you to be in holy conduct and godliness, looking for and hastening the coming of the day of God, on account of which the heavens will be destroyed by burning, and the elements will melt with intense heat! But according to His promise we are looking for new heavens and a new earth, in which righteousness dwells.

Therefore, beloved, since you look for these things, be diligent to be found by Him in peace, spotless and blameless. (2 Peter 3:10–14)

What sort of people ought we to be in holy conduct and godliness! When Sir Walter Raleigh laid his new coat on the ground so that Queen Elizabeth might be able to walk without getting her shoes dirty, he knew that there is no price too great for royalty. Whatever he could do to honor the queen of England should be done. And whatever we can do to honor the King of kings, should be done *now*. And with all that is within us.

The curtain of this earthly drama will close, but it will open in eternity. What we encounter there will have been determined, to some degree, by the life we lived on this earth. Only in this life can we impact the kind of eternity we shall enjoy. *For we are becoming today, the person we will be throughout all of eternity.*

"Behold, I am coming quickly, and My reward is with Me, to render to every man according to what he has done" (Revelation 22:12).

Even so come, Lord Jesus!

## NOTES

1. Iosif Ton, "Suffering, Martyrdom and Rewards in Heaven" (Th.D. diss., Evangelische Theologische Faculteit, Heverlee/Leuben, Belgie, 1996).

2. Randy Alcorn, *Money, Possessions and Eternity* (Wheaton, Ill.: Tyndale, 989), 157.

3. Joseph Dillow, *The Reign of the Servant Kings* (Miami: Schoettle, 1992), 563.

# CHAPTER TEN

# THE GREAT WHITE THRONE JUDGMENT

When I was a teenager, I developed a fervor for the game of Monopoly™. I would try to buy the most expensive property and, if lucky, find my opponent paying a hefty fee for his brief sojourn on Boardwalk. But when one of us was bankrupt, we just put all the fake money and deeds back into the box. The game was over.

Is that what life is all about? Is it true that when we breathe our last everything just gets put back into the box and the game is over? Is the bumper sticker right when it says, "The person with the most toys wins"?

No. Life is an *eternal* game. When it's over here, you and I will be tenderly laid into a box, but the game we played here will continue into the life beyond. We will have to meet God. Death is not a thick wall, but a soft, yielding curtain through which we cannot see, but a curtain that beckons us nevertheless.

This book has been dedicated to a study of the

judgment seat of Christ to which all Christians will be summoned. However, there is another judgment that will also be compulsory. In it the names of all those who have not received Jehovah's forgiveness will be called into account.

The Bible describes it:

> And I saw a great white throne and Him who sat upon it, from whose presence earth and heaven fled away, and no place was found for them. And I saw the dead, the great and the small, standing before the throne, and books were opened; and another book was opened, which is the book of life; and the dead were judged from the things which were written in the books, according to their deeds. And the sea gave up the dead which were in it, and death and Hades gave up the dead which were in them; and they were judged, every one of them according to their deeds. And death and Hades were thrown into the lake of fire. This is the second death, the lake of fire. And if anyone's name was not found written in the book of life, he was thrown into the lake of fire. (Revelation 20:11–15)

We picture the scene: host beyond host, rank behind rank. The millions among the nations of the world, all crowded together in the presence of the One who sits upon the throne, the One who looks intently at each individual.

We are accustomed to human judges; we know their partial and imperfect verdicts. In the presence of the Almighty, all previous judgments are rendered useless. Many men and women acquitted on earth before a human judge will now be found guilty before God. Men who have been accustomed to perks, special privileges, and legal representation now stand as naked in the presence of God. To their horror they are judged by a standard that is light-years beyond them: The standard is God Himself. Little wonder they feel what one writer calls "unfamiliar awfulness."

## A DESCRIPTION OF THE PLAINTIFFS

For the first time in their lives they stand in the presence of unclouded righteousness. They will be asked questions for which they know the answer. Their lives are present before them; unfortunately, they will be doomed to a painful, eternal existence.

What do we notice as we look at this scene?

### Their Diversity

These multitudes standing before the throne are diverse in size. "I saw the dead, the great and the small, standing before the throne" (v. 12). Lives separate on earth come together here: the attorney and the storekeeper, the farmer and the king. Those who lived a private life on earth awake in a realm in which human differences do not matter. The dead of all the ages stand together: black, white, yellow, brown.

There is diversity in time periods and civilizations. "The sea gave up the dead which were in it, and death and Hades gave up the dead which were in them" (v. 13). We think of those who died before Christ came to earth, those who rejected the God of Abraham, Isaac, and Jacob. Then we think of those who lived since the time of Christ, but have treated Him with benign indifference.

We think of Asia with its teeming millions. We think of the country of China, of Japan, Russia, and all of

Europe. We can visualize the United States, and Central and South America. Here are people who lived during the time of the patriarchs as well as those who lived during the days of Abraham Lincoln and John Kennedy.

Not one can beg for a postponement of the court date. Every individual feels that his own soul is immortal; he knows that his existence is what is most important to him. And now it is too late to change his destiny.

This multitude is diverse in its religions. We see Buddhists, Muslims, Hindus, Protestants, and Catholics. We see those who believed in one God and those who believed in many gods. We see those who refused to believe in any God at all. We see those who believed in meditation as a means of salvation and those who believed that doing good deeds was the path to eternal life. We see the moral and the immoral, the priest as well as the minister, the nun as well as the missionary.

## Their Common Experience

The books are thrown wide open and the past is recalled. Details long since forgotten are brought to light. The good, the bad, and the ugly. Many have a litany of good deeds: acts of charity, love, and sacrifice. There is the priest who conscientiously visited the people of his parish standing next to the Protestant minister who expended his life to help the poor and spread justice. There is the poor beggar and the wealthy raja.

Their good works will be carefully recounted, but none will have enough for admittance into heaven. But the good deeds done will make their punishment in the lake of fire more bearable. They will be judged on the basis of what they did with what they knew, or should have known; thus hell will not be the same for everyone.

How accurate will the judgment be? Jonathan Edwards says that it will be meticulous. Sinners will wish they had done just a little less evil that their punishment would be slightly more tolerable; pornographers will wish they had published fewer magazines; control freaks will wish they had been less angry and hurtful; abortionists will wish they had killed fewer pre-born infants. All of this would adjust the degree of punishment at least a bit.

> Though the mills of God grind slowly
> Yet they grind exceedingly small;
> Though with patience He stands waiting
> With exactness He grinds all.
> —Friedrich von Logau, "Retribution"
> Trans. Henry Wadsworth Longfellow

Justice is symbolized on courthouses by the figure of a blindfolded woman with scales in her hand; the point to be made is that she deals impartially, without reference to the parties involved. However, with God it is different: He judges with eyes that are wide open, eyes as of fire that can penetrate the most hardened criminal. He knows not only the individuals, but their parents, brothers, and sisters; He sees the opportunities they had and takes into account their predicament. Justice is carefully administered. Nothing will be overlooked.

## Their Common Destination

Why do the good people and the bad share a common fate? Alas, the good people were not good enough! The requirement to enter heaven is that they be as good as God, and no one qualifies. Even the most devoted religious persons will discover that they fall short of the glory of God.

In addition to the book containing a list of their deeds, there is a second book called the Book of Life. Symbolically, this book is checked from top to bottom, but none of those who are here have their names written there. If their names had been in it, those fortunate souls would already be in heaven appearing at the judgment seat of Christ (discussed in the earlier chapters of this book).

We read, "And if anyone's name was not found written in the book of life, he was thrown into the lake of fire" (Revelation 20:15). They must go obediently into outer darkness. The words of Dante, long since forgotten, come to mind, "All hope abandon, ye who enter here!"

Is the lake of fire a just sentence for those who find themselves in this frightful predicament? What about those who have a raft of good deeds to show for their sojourn here on earth? Does it not appear as if the punishment is greater than the crime warrants?

We must proceed cautiously.

What if it is true, as Jonathan Edwards says, that the greatness of the sin is determined by the greatness of the being against whom it is committed? If so, then even the smallest sin is a serious affront to God. Hell exists because unbelievers are eternally guilty. No human being's suffering can ever be a payment for sin. If human suffering could erase sin, then the lake of fire would eventually end.

Also, keep in mind that the unbelievers will be judged "according to their deeds" (vv. 12, 13). This means that they will be judged fairly; the person who never heard of Christ will be punished more leniently than the person who consciously rejected Him. The good person will be punished less severely than the criminal.

If a man grew up without an understanding of the gospel, this will be taken into account: He will be fairly judged. Blame will also be equitably distributed to his parents, who did not teach the child when he was growing up. Parents, grandparents, opportunities, and handicaps—all of this will be relevant to the final verdict.

To our way of thinking, hell might be considered unjust. But we are not asked to make up the rules by which the game of life is played. Since this is God's universe, He runs it according to His eternal purposes. We must bow to His authority, believing that He does all things well.

## WHAT THE PLAINTIFFS LACKED

What binds these millions of people together is the common view that they will be accepted by God on the basis of their goodness. Virtually all the religions of the world teach that if we live moral lives, if we treat our neighbor with respect and "do the best we can," we will be able to save ourselves. The specifics may vary, but the bottom line is the same. What these people lack is the righteousness that God requires for entry into heaven.

The problem, as I have already mentioned, is that we have to be as good as God to get to enjoy eternity with Him. And since that is impossible, our only hope is to trust Christ, who died so that we might be saved by His merit. In other words, when we believe on

Christ, His righteousness is credited to our account so that legally we are declared to be as perfect as God. Thus, while millions languish in the lake of fire, millions of others who have placed their trust in Christ alone will be enjoying the bliss of heaven.

It would be a mistake to think that those who appear at the Great White Throne Judgment are punished with a different standard than Christians who are enjoying heaven. God is just; He must exact the same from every sinner.

Here is the big difference: Christ bore the wrath of God on behalf of those who believe in Him. He, as the God-man, personally took the punishment of God so that those who believe in Him will be exempt from the lake of fire. Either we must personally bear infinite punishment for our sins or else our sins have to be laid upon an infinite being, namely, Christ. Either way, God is eminently just.

This explains why only those who believe in Christ will be spared the eternal wrath of God. His suffering accomplished in a few hours what purely human suffering can never do. Christ is our sin-bearer, our shelter, our Savior. He forgives us and reconciles us to God. "There is therefore now no condemnation for those who are in Christ Jesus" (Romans 8:1).

If you have never personally believed in Him, or if you are unsure whether you have, here is prayer you can pray that will affirm your desire to believe.

Dear God,
I know that I am a sinner. I cannot save myself from my sins. I also know that I deserve Your judgment. At this moment, as best as I know how, I transfer my faith to Christ alone. I receive His death on the cross in my behalf. I am grateful that He bore my pun-

ishment, and I now accept His sacrifice for myself. I thank You that Christ died and rose again from the dead and ascended into heaven in triumph. Today I receive Him as my personal Savior. "But as many as received Him, to them He gave the right to become children of God, even to those who believe in His name" (John 1:12).

Thank You for hearing me. Amen.

If you have prayed this prayer in faith, God will confirm your decision through His promises and the work of the Holy Spirit in your heart. You have now entered the family of God, with all the rights and privileges that pertain. You will appear at the *Bema,* the judgment seat of Christ, rather than the judgment at the Great White Throne.

Throughout all of eternity we will sing:

> Great and marvelous are Thy works,
> O Lord God, the Almighty;
> Righteous and true are Thy ways,
> Thou King of the nations.
> Who will not fear, O Lord, and glorify Thy name?
> For Thou alone art holy;
> For all the nations will come and worship before Thee,
> For Thy righteous acts have been revealed.
>
> (Revelation 15:3–4)

All glory to God alone, both now and forever.

# Be Sure to Pick Up
# The Entire Eternity Series

One minute after you slip behind the parted curtain, you will either be enjoying a personal welcome from Christ or catching your first glimpse of gloom as you have never know it. Either way, your future will be irrevocably fixed and eternally unchangeable. Don't spend more time planning your trip to Europe than you do preparing for your eternal home.

**ISBN 978-0-8024-6305-0**

Is it possible to know, in this life, where you will spend eternity? In this concise and powerful book, respected pastor and author Erwin Lutzer explains why you can know, even now, where you will be after death. He inists that many who expect to enter heaven will discover that they were sadly mistaken. But it is not too late for those who are still living to choose the right path—and know it.

**ISBN 978-0-8024-2719-9**

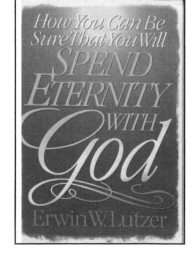